PERCEPTION vs. REALITY

IN YOUTH SPORTS

==========

Understanding the
Real World of Kids and Sports
*Through the Experiences of
Successful Athletes*

J A PATTERSON

PERCEPTION vs. REALITY IN YOUTH SPORTS
Understanding the Real World of Kids and Sports
Through the Experiences of Successful Athletes

ISBN: 978-0-692-20562-4

This book is available at special quantity discounts for
use in fundraising, education, coaching, promotion, etc.
For information, contact:

customerservice@real-worldpublishing.com

Real World Publishing: 40 E. Chicago Ave., Suite 146
                         Chicago, IL   60611

Cover Design by: Daliborka Mijailovic

THIS BOOK IS DEDICATED TO ALL OF THE YOUTH SPORTS VOLUNTEERS WHO GENEROUSLY GIVE (AND HAVE GIVEN) THEIR TIME, ENERGY, MONEY, PATIENCE, AND WISDOM THROUGH THE YEARS.

YOU ARE PRICELESS.

CONTENTS

PREFACE

I have written a book that I wish I had read when my kids were young, playing their way through many different sports experiences. It would have helped me better understand how to support them, and I could have used the examples in this book for insight when situations came up. This book would have enlightened us all.

While my athletically involved boys played on, I co-managed a youth track program for over 10 years; I volunteered in "almost every sport" at one time or another; and I watched as one son played Division I college golf (now competing as a professional).

I have also had a very long career as a researcher and writer. And, because of my ability to be objective, I was hired by Fortune 500 companies to observe and report what was going on in their respective worlds. My work often required me to explain to my clients: *"Based on the research, your 'real world' is not necessarily what you think it is."* And that is exactly what I am trying to say to both parents and kids with this book.

I know youth sports. However, I have not written about my opinions: this book is built around research, and is different from the many helpful youth sports books already written. Incorporating anecdotes and observations about the young athletic lives of successful athletes—and quoting the opinions of experts—I want to bring reality to the surface, and address the many false perceptions that float throughout the youth sports community. I want to shine a light on: what it takes for kids to enjoy the youth sports experience; how kids can find fulfillment in athletic activity—at any level; and I want to give parents insight about the role that they play in this important aspect of their childrens' lives.

This book was written for parents and older children to read. (Parents of young children can relay the stories to them and use the book as a teaching tool.)

INTRODUCTION

A TRUE STORY: During a youth track meet, the boys' mile race with 7- and 8-year-olds was underway (4 laps around the track), and there was one overweight boy in the race who was very, very slow. This boy was eventually passed by *every single one* of his fellow runners, but he really wasn't aware of that. As a result, he thought he was on his last lap when the others were—so he stopped at the finish line when everyone else did. But he, *by himself*, had one more lap to run in order to complete the race.

When this boy was given that information at the finish line, his shoulders slumped dramatically; but he immediately put one foot ahead of the other and started to run again. It looked like he was dragging the weight of the world along with him, trudging along more slowly than before; but he kept running—*all by himself, on a big track, in front of hundreds of people!*

With only one person running, the crowd became aware of what was going on, and everyone stood and cheered in support of the incredible perseverance of this lonely runner. Then, as soon as the cheering began, the boy's shoulders straightened ... his pace picked up ... he held his head high ... and he ended up *sprinting* toward the finish line—to the roar of the crowd!

I will never forget this young man.

This story represents the true essence of youth sports. It represents the reasons I am passionate about this topic. Participating in youth sports can have an immense, positive impact on a child—given the proper perspective of the kids and/or the parents. Nevertheless, there is no question that youth sports can have a significantly negative impact on kids—given the wrong perspective by the kids and/or the parents.

Some of the "perceptions" that many parents and kids have about youth sports are somewhat misguided, but everyone's perceptions are different. I can't predict which ones, if any, might be affected by what is in this book. Just read about the real-world of athletes and see what happens to your perceptions/reality.

Perhaps the information provided here will bring up the expectations of some kids and parents; perhaps it will bring down the expectations of others. It is also possible that reading this book will relieve you, the parent, of guilt—if you have fear that you don't cheer loudly enough, show up for enough games, or don't know what to say to your athlete in certain situations. On the other hand ... you may feel guilty if you have yelled at a coach, criticized your child's performance, or if you gave up too early on your child's ability to move forward in a sport.

For you, the young athlete: It is possible that reading this book will allow you to enjoy your sports more, take some of the pressure off of yourself—and just have fun. And if you really want to get better at any sport, this book will give you insight into why you might have to work a little harder, and persevere.

PERCEPTION vs. REALITY
IN YOUTH SPORTS

==========

Understanding the
Real World of Kids and Sports
Through the Experiences of
Successful Athletes

THERE'S GOOD.
THERE'S BAD.

During a light conversation with a young man who had been married for a few years, the subject of children came up—and he said he and his wife didn't know whether they wanted to have kids or not. He followed up with these exact words: *We don't know if we want to get into all that weird stuff about kids and sports and everything...........*

Is the "perception" of youth sports really that bad these days?

Anyone involved in youth sports would agree that the good aspects outweigh the bad.....by far! Nevertheless, most would also acknowledge that sports aren't for every child; and not every child's experience is a positive one.

Blogger and mom of four kids, Allison Tate, pointed that out when she wrote about one of her children who has no interest in playing sports: "I know, though, that no matter how much he resembles the dream of Pop Warner coaches everywhere, my son is not that kid. That, we have decided, is just fine." She also refers to the book, *The Story of Ferdinand* by Munro Leaf, to explain that "there is a place in the world for the Ferdinands." (From *HuffingtonPost.com*)

Whether you're currently involved in youth sports or just considering it..............*read on.*

THE BENEFITS OF YOUTH SPORTS

FUN ...
THE OPPORTUNITY TO *JUST PLAY*

Kids have a lot of fun playing organized sports! In fact, according to more than one study, "fun" is the number one reason they like playing sports. And the word "fun" still comes up when successful athletes are interviewed or profiled. These mature athletes never forget the fun they had as children playing sports. In fact, many refer back to the fun of their childhoods when describing something good that happens to them during their adult sports careers.

Former NHL great Wayne Gretzky, in an interview in *USA Today*, talked about the fun he had in the backyard skating rink his father built for him as a kid. He said, "I think the great athletes go back to their childhood. They go back to their love of the game. It never left me. Even when I became a champion, I always had the same feeling I had in the back yard." Similarly, NASCAR's Jeff Gordon told *USA Today*, "Being able to see that checkered flag, it reminds me of being a kid. And that moment of joy comes out."

When MLB pitcher Dontrelle Willis was asked by a young reader in a *Sports Illustrated Kids* interview, *How much fun is major league baseball?* he responded, "More than you can imagine, to be honest. Just the anticipation of the game and whatever surprises there may be. You never know what's in store. It's like Christmas Day, 162 days a year."

Sports Illustrated writer Steve Rushin's article on this topic contains quotes from professional athletes referring to the fun of their childhood sports experiences. "I felt like a little kid, when my mom took me to Toys 'R Us," said baseball's C C Sabathia, after making the playoffs. "I felt like a kid playing his first Little League game. I was so happy to be in there," said Detroit Tigers rookie Brandon Inge, after he hit his first major league home run. "I felt like a little kid, running around in the puddles," said New England Revolution midfielder Steve Ralston, about making a game-winning goal after a thunderstorm. And two different professional quarterbacks, Mark Rypien and Rodney Peete, were quoted saying the same thing after returning from a long layoff: "I felt like a kid again."

Sports psychologist Dr. Bob Rotella says in his book, *The Golfer's Mind*, "Trust me. The players I know who have the best minds also have the most fun playing golf. They understand that it is, in the end, a game. They have a ball finding out how good they can be at it."

Landon Donovan, considered the best professional soccer player America has produced, told the *Los Angeles Times* that, as a kid, "We just loved going outside and playing. That was all I knew about soccer: going outside and playing with my friends."

Writer Ben Bolch of the *Los Angeles Times* wrote a moving article about the impact of football on the teenage boys in a juvenile detention center named Camp Kilpatrick. In the article, the team's coach, Derek Ayres, explained; "It [football] means a lot to them because it gives them an opportunity to step into an environment that allows them to be kids again."

PHYSICAL HEALTH

The findings of a USC/NIH study analyzing activity data on over 3,000 children indicated that normal weight children get 16 more minutes of physical activity a day than overweight children. *Only 16 minutes!* Clearly, any amount of activity is better than no activity. Playing any type of youth sport will go a long way in keeping children active and in relatively good physical shape, particularly where weight is concerned. It doesn't take intense participation to keep weight off of children.

Most importantly, experts agree that active youth are more likely to become active adults, and that the mentality developed by being active as a child can be "imprinted" for a lifetime. Also, a child with a normal weight is more likely to develop into an adult with a normal weight.

Former New York Giants defensive end Michael Strahan has admitted that he was fat when he was a kid because he "just sat around and ate." He was often teased by his brothers, so he decided to get fit by watching Jane Fonda's workout video, and has since declared, "I set the quarterback sack record because of Jane Fonda."

POSITIVE INFLUENCE ON ACADEMICS

Studies consistently indicate that young athletes are:

- ✗ more likely to enjoy school.
- ✗ less likely to drop out of school.
- ✗ more likely to get higher grades.
- ✗ more likely to attend college.
- ✗ likely to have greater occupational/career success.

Organized sports programs at the middle school and high school level generally require a certain level of academic performance for participation. That keeps some students more focused on academics: if they want to play sports, they have to keep their grades up. And as they get older and perhaps hope to play college sports, athletes learn that there are many colleges that require a high level of academic success before they will consider an athlete for sports participation—regardless of their athletic skills.

LSU running back Kenny Hilliard was a star high school football player, but didn't have the reading skills he needed to graduate from high school. He knew that he had to improve his reading if he wanted to go any further in football, so he participated in a program for elementary school kids that taught reading skills, and he had to attend classes with 3rd graders. He did it, and ended up loving reading so much that he turned into a B- student in high school.

It is important for both kids and parents to recognize that there truly is time in a young athlete's day for both sports and school;

the demands of sports participation should not be used as an excuse for weak academic performance. In fact, many very successful athletes managed to keep their grades very high (close to 4.0). Following are just a few of the many:

Toby Gerhart (NFL)
Ryan Fitzpatrick (NFL)
Tim Tebow (NFL)
Brad Ausmus (MLB)
Stephen Strasburg (MLB)
Colin Kaepernick (NFL)
Emeka Okafor (NBA)
Alex Smith (NFL)
Craig Breslow (NFL)
Shane Battier (NBA)
Drew Brees (NFL)
George Parros (NHL)

NFL quarterback Christian Ponder finished with a GPA of 3.73 at Florida State, graduated in 2½ years and then earned an MBA. Said Ponder in an interview on website *THEBIGLEAD.com*: "Academics has always been important to my family. My parents have always pushed me to do well in school not knowing what's going to happen in football."

Professional softball star Jessica Mendoza has said, "When I talk to girls, I always emphasize *student* before *athlete*. I've got a master's degree from Stanford ... I just haven't used it yet."

Major League pitcher Ross Ohlendorf played college ball at Princeton after excelling at both basketball and baseball in high school. When graduating from Princeton, he received the school's George Mueller Award for *combining high scholarly achievement in the study of engineering with quality performance in intercollegiate athletics*, and he was named the "third smartest athlete" by *Sporting News* in 2010 (behind Craig Breslow and Myron Rolle).

NBA star Vince Carter has said that he signed a contract with his mother before going to college, promising her that he would earn his diploma no matter what happened with basketball—and he did graduate.

NFL player Denard Robinson rejected the more typical path of many football players who leave college early to train for the NFL draft, as he was determined to graduate first. As told in a *Yahoo!Sports* article, Denard said, "I was never going to do that because I wouldn't have graduated. It was the dream of my family to see me graduate. I'm going to be the first in my family to graduate from a four-year school." In order to do that, Robinson had to work even harder than his upcoming draft competition, and he sacrificed.

Finally ... one of the more impressive standard-bearers for the importance of education—for both young athletes and non-athletes—is NBA superstar Amar'e Stoudemire. He is using his athlete role model status to encourage kids to read, by writing sports-oriented books for them that will provide entertaining reading, and will also teach them about character.

DEVELOPMENT OF SOCIAL SKILLS ... SOCIAL INTERACTION

Being part of a team or a group is an important reason for many kids to want to play a sport. Kids widen their circle of friends through sports, they learn how to interact socially with others, and they learn how to actively participate in social groups.

Whether it is fair or not, research studies have also suggested that athletic kids tend to be generally more popular than non-athletic kids. For example, a study published in the "Journal of Sport Behavior" tied confidence in athletic ability to popularity, and the research suggested that giving children even a minimal level of athletic skill helps their feelings of happiness and social well-being. It was also found that athletes don't necessarily have to be good athletes to gain the popularity benefit.

Former NFL star Clay Matthews, Jr. has described how being an athlete when he was young gave him an easy entry into new schools when his family frequently moved. Said Matthews, "I could go and play football right away and have 35 - 40 friends immediately."

There are many kids, however, who might be a little shy, awkward, or stressed when involved in team or group activities. Parents of these kids often wonder what to do about their children's involvement in sports, and question whether the child should even play sports or not. As an alternative to team sports, these kids often thrive in individual sports such as track/cross country, golf, tennis, etc. They enjoy the independence of not having to interact on an ongoing basis with groups of loud, overwhelming kids; but they still experience the sense of belonging to a group—on a low-key basis. (The topic of team sports vs. individual sports is discussed in a later chapter.)

YOUTH SPORTS AS THE "GREAT EQUALIZER"

Another social benefit of participation in sports is that it bridges the gaps that often exist between kids who are of a different race, size, personality, intelligence level, etc.

ESPNW.com wrote about Lizette Salas, the first Mexican-American woman on the LPGA tour, who earned her tour card in 2012 at the age of 22. Playing golf was not a common activity at her high school, which was 82% socio-economically disadvantaged, or in her neighborhood, which was predominantly Mexican-American. But she started playing golf because she "hung around" the local golf course where her father worked. Graduating from USC through a golf scholarship, she was the first person in her family to get a college diploma. And now, she says, her thoughts on her Mexican-American status in golf are: "Now I know it's just about putting a ball in the hole. You do that well and it doesn't matter what your background is. The game is what people remember."

In a *Sports Illustrated Kids* article, former NFL star Hines Ward talked about growing up bi-racial (Korean and African American): "So growing up and in high school, it was tough. But for me, I really found my identity through sports. Once I got a ball in my hands, it really wasn't about race anymore. That made it a little easier."

The late Willye White, an Olympic track and field medalist, and a member of the USA Track & Field Hall of Fame, was raised by her grandparents in Mississippi before the Civil Rights movement. In speaking of the impact sports had on her life, she told *Sports Illustrated for Women*, "Before my first Olympics, I thought the whole world consisted of cross burnings and lynchings. The Olympic movement taught me not to judge a person by the color of their skin but by the contents of their hearts. I am who I am because of my participation in sports."

In his Hall of Fame induction speech, former NFL star Michael Irvin talked about his love for all aspects of the game of football, but he particularly singled out his favorite movie, *Remember the Titans*, as representing the impact that football has on almost anyone involved. Referring to the movie, he said, "The game of football unites a whole town—black, white, old, young, rich and poor. And it happens every year around this time, in NFL locker rooms and NFL stadiums. So don't tell me it's just a game."

Much has been written about how NBA star Jeremy Lin has inspired Asian-American kids to consider pursuing basketball, as well as other sports. In an *Orange County Register* article, award-winning sportswriter Kevin Ding, who is Taiwanese-American, quotes his cousin's son, a 13-year old basketball player, and also a Taiwanese-American: "He [Lin] proves that Asians aren't all just nerdy and smart. Asians can be just as athletically as good as anyone. ... We all need a reason to hope, but especially kids."

ESCAPE/RELIEF FROM DIFFICULT CIRCUMSTANCES

The professional athletic world is filled with stories of the redemption and salvation that participation in youth sports provided many of those who went on to become successful athletes.

Sports can keep kids away from the temptations of trouble by demanding responsibility and time commitments from them, and by making them accountable to something or someone. Participation in sports activities also takes kids' bodies and souls out of what might be a stressful world for them at home or at school. Sports gives them something fun and happy on which to focus, and gives kids a sense of purpose. It also gives many kids a feeling of family that they, otherwise, might not have. Sometimes a coach even becomes the father/mother figure they don't have.

The owner of a Philadelphia factory clearly recognized the value of sports activities when he asked a friend to organize a youth football program so that the neighborhood kids would stop breaking his factory windows. He believed that the kids were just restless and bored, and attacking his factory was "sport" to them; so he wanted to find something to keep them busy. This league soon became the Pop Warner Football League, which thrives today. (The League was named after a legendary football coach from Temple University.)

Though there are so many incredibly inspiring athletes' stories regarding personal escapes from difficult circumstances, only a small number can be told here. They follow:

Former high school football player Antwone Shepherd told sportswriter Bill Plaschke that after a difficult childhood, and an attempted suicide as a teenager, "I found a place to put my anger" after joining the football team. I've never had a home like this," said Shepherd. And in response, his coach, Jimmy Nolan, commented, "It's what everybody in this game preaches, isn't it? It's never really about football; it's always about life, right?"

NFL draft pick Brandon Williams told *Yahoo!Sports* that while growing up in poverty, his job working with a portable toilet company motivated him to work hard toward a sports career. Said Williams, "Every time I was doing that, I said to myself, 'I gotta work harder, I'm not doing this the rest of my life.' It motivated me to get better."

Football pro Todd Williams was homeless at the age of 15 because no family members could care for him; so he left school and lived on the streets in Miami for a short time. As he told *Sports Illustrated Kids*, he was "bitter and angry," and he admitted that he stole clothes, slept in trash bins, and broke into motels for shelter. Eventually going back to high school, he tried out for the football team when he was a sophomore and quickly became an All-State tackle and an All-American. As a result, Williams earned a football scholarship to Florida State and was chosen in the 7th round of the 2003 NFL draft.

In the article, Williams gave credit to football for "giving him a way to work out his complicated and angry feelings, relieving him of his bitterness, and allowing him to take pride in how far he has come."

In a *New York Post* article about Football Hall of Famer Curtis Martin, Martin claimed, "Football saved my life. I don't know where I would be. I don't know if I'd be alive if I hadn't played football." He added, "Football was like my basic training for life. I've learned how to work hard, how to commit, so many things I didn't know how to do until I had football in my life."

In a *Los Angeles Times* interview, the NFL's Jeremy Ross described how he was in and out of group homes and failing classes until he decided he wanted to play football. He had to get his grades up, and he did—eventually becoming captain of the varsity team. Said Ross, "It's kind of hard to come from the bottom and work all the way up. I have a long way to go. Without my team, I couldn't do it. They look over me. I look over them. This is my family."

Olympic gold medalist Michael Phelps found refuge at his local pool, escaping the challenges at home and at school—his parents fighting at home, school bullies who made fun of his appearance, his ADHD ... Regarding those kids who taunted him; "I kind of laugh at it now," said Phelps to *Yahoo!Sports*. "I think it made me stronger going through that." It has also been said that Phelps found the father figure he never had in his coach, Bob Bowman.

Professional golfer Jason Day lost his dad at 11 years old, and admits that he was an alcoholic at 12. Because he was often in trouble and in fistfights, he was sent to a boarding school that had very few recreational options other than golf. He has since said that reading about Tiger Woods at a young age motivated him to work on golf, and his golf coach mentored him as a father-like figure.

A *USA Today* profile of Olympic runner Lopez Lomong dramatically describes his having spent 10 years of his childhood in a refugee camp as one of the "Lost Boys of Sudan," before he arrived in the United States and was adopted by an American family. In the article, Lomong describes how running impacted him: "Running saved my life ... and kept me going in the refugee camp. It kept me away from hunger, because I would go for a run."

SKILL DEVELOPMENT

Markus Burden was picked randomly out of the college basketball crowd at Ball State University, and given the chance to shoot a basketball from mid-court. If he made the basket he would win a semester's tuition. And though Burden had only ever played "rec center basketball," he made the shot!

The moral of that story is that whether or not a child who participates in youth sports goes on to play that sport in high school, college, or the pros, he or she will have an understanding of sports, and will have athletic skills that will be carried with him/her for life. And ... who knows? Your child could do what Markus Burden did—and win college tuition.

An anonymous blog contained a commentary by an Asian-American writer who wrote about the success of Jeremy Lin; but he also reflected on his own experiences playing basketball as a youth—and what being able to play basketball has meant to him as an adult.

The writer tells how his dad taught him basketball when he was 11 years old, and he made his high school team, but never thought of basketball as an option for his future, because he followed what he called "the typical Asian attitude of studying hard, getting into a good college, and landing a stable job."

Into the essay, he switched emotional gears and went on to say that, "Little did I know, after graduating high school, that basketball is the only constant in my life. I have switched jobs, lived on both coasts, and traveled to various countries. It didn't matter where I went, I always sought leagues to play in and surround myself with people who are passionate about the game ... there is always a game to be played."

(From Getontheline.wordpress.com: "Inside the mind of a (rec) basketball player.")

DISCIPLINE ...
THE IMPORTANCE OF HARD WORK

Athletes learn the importance of discipline, either through the requirements of practice, or by the demands they make of themselves. Unfortunately, some kids abandon sports because they don't like the required level of discipline; others stick with sports and thrive as they gain a sense of order and accomplishment.

Former professional basketball star and U.S. State Senator Bill Bradley wrote about the lessons he learned through basketball in his book, *The Values of the Game:* "The by-product of countless hours of practice was a sense of discipline that carried over into every aspect of my life. Knowing that hard work, practice and dedication can lead to success prepared me for some of life's challenges."

Ammar Moussa, once the top-ranked high school cross country runner in the country, was a trouble maker in middle school. He changed after taking up cross country in high school, and he has said that the rigorous demands of cross country taught him discipline, helped him gain focus in the rest of his life, and helped him become a better teammate.

Country music star Kenny Chesney has talked about the impact football had on his music career. He told *Parade Magazine* that he went out for football his junior year in high school, played as a wide receiver, and instantly fell in love with the game. Although he ended up being a professional country music singer, not an athlete, he explained, "It all started for me on that field. Football taught me how hard you had to work to achieve something." And, though he didn't start playing guitar and performing until after high school, he credits his high school football experience with providing him "the same principle of focus that I had learned playing football."

As former ATP Tour tennis professional Hank Pfister says in an article he wrote about youth tennis; "The point of sports is to teach the process of learning, which is to practice, prepare, compete, think on your own, adjust to mistakes, re-apply new skills and knowledge at the next competitive opportunity ... all of which leads to improvement."

TEAMWORK

Any adults who have been out in the real world understand the importance of teamwork, and the need to know how to work effectively within groups. And there is probably no more effective way for a growing child to learn the lessons of teamwork than to be on an athletic team. The lessons are sometimes subtle, sometimes bold, but are, plentiful and everlasting.

The Positive Coaching Alliance claims in their article, "Lessons Learned from the 2010 Giants World Series Victory," that teamwork is generally more important than talent. They explain that when the baseball season began [before the Series], the Giants were not expected to go so far. In fact, the managers and players called themselves "a bunch of misfits," and most baseball fans agreed that they didn't appear to have the talent to win a World Series. However, the article explains that the team won the World Series that year because all of the Giants were "playing for the team," and that the role of hero changed from game to game.

A high school teammate and best friend of NBA star Dwight Howard told *USA Today* that, though Howard was already a superstar on the high school team, "Dwight was humble ... he didn't have an agenda like 'I have to get my 30 [points] or get my 30 rebounds.' He did what he needed to do to win. He made the extra pass, got rebounds. I looked out for him, and he looked out for me and everybody else. Everybody was equal."

As part of his Hall of Fame speech, former pro football star Emmitt Smith clearly expressed his respect for teamwork when he called out his former teammate, Daryl Johnston, and touchingly said, "You sacrificed so much for me. People don't understand what it took to be a fullback in our system, the sacrifices you made not simply with your body, but your whole spirit. You took care of me as though you were taking care of your little brother. Without you, without you, I know today would not have been possible."

Jackie Elliott, a Montana Gatorade Soccer Player of the Year, told *USA Today* about a key benefit of being on a sports team. As she explained, "Being on a team has a huge impact on who you are because you have to learn how to react in certain situations, together. You can't just do whatever you want, you have to do what's best for the group."

LEADERSHIP ...
ROLE MODEL RESPONSIBILITY

Has it ever been determined whether great leaders are born or made? Hard to say where that philosophical argument stands in the 21st century, but leadership certainly comes to the forefront in sports. Some children clearly show indications of natural leadership skills and traits at an early age, and sports participation allows them to uncover those inherent traits, and to develop them. Participation in youth sports can also can teach children leadership skills that they might not have ever learned, otherwise.

Former NFL quarterback Tim Tebow has often talked about the responsibilities of being an athlete and role model, and he even has a framed verse on his wall that says, "Little eyes are watching you."

Gordon Hayward, college basketball star on the 2010 NCAA finals Butler team—and 9th overall pick in the NBA draft—told *USA Today* that Steve Nash was his key role model growing up because "he [Nash] played with so much passion. He always got his teammates involved. I thought he played basketball the right way."

The guardian and coach of a young LeBron James made him the assistant coach of the 4th grade team, when he was only in the 5th grade. He explained that move in a *SportsIllustrated.com* article: "Acting as an assistant coach gave LeBron his understanding of what it meant to be a role model. All of the fourth graders wanted to be just like him, so he began doing what he felt was right ... taking pride at such an early age in his responsibility of being a role model to others."

By all accounts, Roberto Garza Jr. was an unlikely prospect for the NFL. The son of hard-working Mexican immigrants, he grew up in a town of only 2,000, made up mostly of Latino farmers. He didn't even speak much English until he left home after high school. After being drafted by the NFL in the 4th round, Garza became a hero in his small town, and he even has a street named after him. Because of his success, the people in his town are said to have a new sense of "anything is possible," and he is the "role model for countless children wanting to aspire to anything."

RESILIENCE ... BOUNCING BACK

It is probably safe to say that "resilience" is near the top of the list of the traits parents want children to acquire. They will need it throughout the years, and even before they get out of high school. What better way for kids to learn resilience than through participation in a youth sport activity where, if they get knocked down, they have to get up; if they get critiqued, they have to try to improve; and if they make mistakes, they have to learn to forget them.

As a commencement speaker, Olympic gold medalist figure skater Michelle Kwan told the audience, "In every great thing we try, there are bound to be disappointments ... I guess that's why the first lesson they give you in skating is how to fall. Everyone takes a spill, and the true test is how we recover."

California's Westlake High School has a healthy sports rivalry with another school in the area, Oaks Christian. When the two schools play football, the game always has a sell-out crowd. In 2010, Westlake High School lost the Division Championship game to Oaks Christian by one point after Westlake kicker, Alex Ball, missed a field goal. Of course, Ball was devastated by his "mistake," and he even considered switching schools after that game—a game he described as "One of the toughest games in my life." But his teammates, schoolmates, and coaches went out of their way to support him—all the way to his eventual acceptance of that one play.

At the start of the next season, Ball told the *Ventura County Star*, "I am glad I missed that kick. It made me train harder." He continued, "I worked on my flaws, worked hard all through the off-season. I came back determined to have a great season." And

Ball did have an exceptional 2011 season, even kicking five field goals in the 2011 "rivalry game" against Oaks Christian. Important to note, as well, is that Ball had such a good season that year that he was named "Top US Kicker" in 2011—having made 19 field goals his senior year!

Former Major League pitcher Jim Abbott is widely known for only having the use of one hand. He now gives motivational speeches and often says that what he learned from baseball, in particular, is that "you might be down now, but you don't know what's going to happen tomorrow." He follows up with a personal example, describing how he once had a game where he surrendered 7 runs and 10 hits in a little over three innings ... and then threw a no-hitter in the very next game he pitched.

GENERAL LIFE LESSONS

Because sports have become intertwined with so much of the way we experience society, children can only gain from having some exposure to the dynamics of athletics. Sports truly are pervasive in our world. For example, just think about the fact that on any given day we are likely to hear (or use) at least one of the many sports phrases and expressions that have found their way into our everyday language, such as:

the ball's in your court ◆ step up to the plate
strike out ◆ down and out ◆ touch base
home court advantage ◆ ground rules ◆ rain check
ballpark estimate ◆ take one for the team
slam dunk ◆ the homestretch ◆ take a victory lap
off to a running start ◆ off-base ◆ play hardball
roll with the punches ◆ out of left field
going for the gold ◆ get a head start
it's a marathon, not a sprint ◆ win hands down
gain the upper hand ◆ throw a curve ball
down to the wire ◆ throw in the towel
right off the bat

On a more individual level, it is touching, enlightening, and motivating to hear athletes talk about what their involvement in sports has meant to them...............

In his Hall of Fame induction speech, the great Deion Sanders described the impact that football had on him. "This game taught me how to be a man. This game taught me if I get knocked down, I've got to get my butt back up. It taught me so much about people, timing, focus, dedication, submitting oneself, sacrificing."

Billy Strean, a professor who studies kids and coaches, has described sports as "a fantastic way to connect with others. You grow. You test yourself. There are so many phenomenal opportunities. And it is inherently enjoyable to get better at something."

Anita Ortega, commander of the largest division of the Los Angeles Police Department, was on a UCLA National Championship basketball team as a point guard. She once told the *Los Angeles Times*, "Athletics, in general, prepared me for this [her job]. Where I grew up, I played a lot of basketball with guys. It taught me about teamwork, confidence ..."

Finally ... given all of the wonderful benefits of youth sports, how can anyone challenge their value in the lives of kids? But, their value is, indeed, being challenged—particularly when it comes to budget cutting in the school systems. Not only are some elementary and middle schools limiting, or completely eliminating, many physical education programs, but even high schools are eliminating certain sports activities. In fact, one entire school district in Texas cancelled all school athletics "so that students would be forced to focus on improving their grades and the overall test results for the district." Really?

THE DOWNSIDE OF YOUTH SPORTS

There are some "not so pleasant" aspects of youth sports that get a lot of attention, and some of you might have concerns. You're not alone. A Blue Cross Blue Shield Association survey found that parents' biggest concerns regarding youth sports are:

1) Use of performance-enhancing supplements and drugs by youngsters (39% of parents)

2) None (20%)

3) Encouraging aggressive behavior among youngsters (16%)

4) Excessive Competitiveness (15%)

5) Frequency of Injuries (10%)

If you are just entering into youth sports, there is no cause for alarm. As with anything else in the media, the negative issues receive more attention than the positive, and a few (bad people) ruin it for the rest of us. The vast majority of adults involved in youth sports are balanced parents and coaches who have only the kids' best interests at heart. (Though there will be a few crazy, out-of-control people, too.) It is unlikely that any of your children will be attacked by a rabid coach, or insulted by an irate parent; and hopefully, none of your children will end up using steroids, or experiencing anything more than a scraped knee or a bruised ego.

Nevertheless ... it is important to address the downside of youth sports in order to give you an objective perspective of what can happen and what you need to be aware of.

INJURIES

According to the U.S. Centers for Disease Control:

✗ More than 3.5 million kids under the age of 14 receive medical treatment for sports injuries each year.

✗ 62% of organized sports-related injuries occur during practice.

✗ High school athletes account for an estimated 2 million injuries and 500,000 doctor visits and 30,000 hospitalizations each year.

Youth sports injuries are a hot topic these days. Injuries do happen, the majority of them are minor and temporary, and the most important consideration with any injury is how to treat it properly—which includes being patient, and giving it time to heal.

Researching sports injuries, I reviewed many studies and articles written about them, and most just make the point that parents, coaches, and kids have to be aware and careful and take reasonable precautions—particularly when it comes to sports practice, and when it comes to equipment.

A recent Ohio State study that examined injury data in nine different sports, in 100 high schools nationwide, determined that, over a two-year period, roughly 15% of all high school sports-related injuries were classified as "severe." (They defined a severe injury as one that resulted in losing three weeks or more of sports participation.) Among those severe injuries, 28% required surgery.

The same study reported that football had the highest injury rate, followed by wrestling, girls' basketball, and girls' soccer. It also indicated that "knees" were the top area of injury, followed by ankles and shoulders; and the most common diagnosis was fractures, followed by ligament sprains.

Interestingly, girls had a higher *severe* injury rate than did boys, even though the *overall* injury rate was higher in boys' sports than girls' sports. Girls' basketball did rank higher in injuries than did boys' basketball, however. (There are no clear-cut explanations for this difference in severity level among girls, but some believe that the adolescent female body responds to physical impact/stress somewhat differently than does the male body, and young teen girls' tendons and ligaments are different.)

The important news is that the CDC claims that more than half of all sports injuries in children are preventable; and there are more and more significant efforts being built around the concept of keeping young athletes safer from injury. One example: a campaign called STOP Sports Injuries (*stopsportsinjuries.org*) has been established by a group of business, sports, and medical leaders to bring the safety message to parents, coaches, and healthcare providers. Through offering education and other resources, they hope to reduce the overall incidence of injuries.

CONCUSSIONS

Concussions are probably the most potentially serious injury that young athletes experience. From recent news reports, it may seem as if every child is getting a concussion every time they go out on a field to practice or play. Concussions do happen, and no youth sports program ignores that reality. Serious effort is being directed toward reducing the number and extent of concussions, sports organizations are changing rules, and equipment makers are improving safety features.

Even at the professional level, concussions are taken much more seriously these days. It is a frequent topic of sports news, and the athletes, themselves, are expressing concern. NFL star Clay Matthews III, for one, acknowledged his change of attitude about concussions when he told the *Acorn* newspaper that he used to consider concussions as a "less serious injury than something like a broken bone," but he knows better now.

Football is not the only youth sport in which concussions occur. While they are most common in football, girls' soccer has the second most concussions, followed by boys' soccer, hockey, and lacrosse. Concussions are also prevalent in the martial arts, and in both girls' and boys' basketball. Baseball and softball players are exposed to concussion risks, particularly when sliding headfirst into a base and hitting a leg or shin guard; and in track and field, pole vaulters are at risk.

The most important consideration with concussions is how they are cared for after they occur. A *USA Today* article cited studies that indicate that as many as 40% of children with concussion injuries return to action pre maturely. As a result, there is a movement among experts in the field to influence coaches and parents to resist the urge to tell young children to "shake it off, tough it out, get back in the game." In addition, most states are individually passing laws that influence how concussions are handled in youth sports activities.

In defense of coaches and parents, however, it is often the kids, themselves, who are so anxious to get back into the game that they are not honest about how they feel after an injury. Kids need clear instructions about how critical the post-injury period is—though it is difficult to make them "get it." For example, even after a high school team watched an NFL report about the seriousness of concussions, one linebacker quoted in a *USA Today* article said, "I can't really see myself missing a game because of a headache." (Obviously, there is a lot of work to do on all fronts.)

OVERUSE INJURIES

The CDC claims that overuse injuries make up nearly half of all the sports injuries of middle school and high school athletes. Also, there has been a five-fold increase in the number of serious shoulder and elbow injuries among youth baseball and softball players since 2000. For young baseball pitchers, in particular, injuries have become more common as these kids pitch with greater intensity, and focus on the pitching position at too young of an age. Experts also point out that more and more young baseball players are playing year-round, instead of only during "baseball season," and that this is completely inappropriate and harmful for the still- developing adolescent.

A study by the American Sports Medicine Institute in Birmingham illustrates that young pitchers who play more than eight months of baseball a year are five times more likely to need surgery later on, as compared to those who pitch no more than 5½ months a year. The same research indicates that Little League pitchers between the ages of 9 and 14 should be limited to 100 innings in a year, and that they should not be throwing curveballs until the age of 14 or 15—because the motion puts too much pressure on the pitcher's elbow.

While most of the arm injuries in young pitchers are temporary, some do need surgery, and some result in permanent damage and reduced arm function. There are even young injuries that are ending future pitching careers completely; but the most alarming development, according to medical experts, is the fact that "Tommy John Surgery" is being performed on a significant number of pitchers even before they get out of high school. (This surgical procedure was typically used only for major league pitchers until the last 10 years or so.)

One of the most prominent examples, among many, is superstar pitcher Steven Strasburg, who had to sit out a large part of the 2012 season due to concern over the wear and tear on his pitching arm—at the ripe old age of 24. Premier sports agent Scott Boras, in a *Washington Post* interview, said of Strasburg: "I saw this coming. I saw all this coming. He was too talented and his body wasn't yet mature. He was so young."

KNEE INJURIES

Knee injuries are also one of the more common injuries in youth sports, and the incidence is increasing. For example, ACL/knee repair used to be somewhat rare in children, but now 1 in 5 ACL surgeries in males is for a youth under the age of 18; and 30% of the ACL surgeries in females are for girls under 18. Girls' knee injuries are particularly common in soccer, and they happen to even the best athletes.

Specialists emphasize that they are quite concerned about these young knee injuries because they are more difficult to treat effectively in kids than they are in adults, and they can have long-lasting effects.

OTHER INJURIES

Hockey injuries in kids are frequent, but most are the common cuts, bruises, broken bones, broken noses, etc. A University of Buffalo study indicated that 66% of youth hockey injuries are caused by accidental contact such as colliding with players, hitting boards, and flying pucks; however, 34% of the injuries are caused by deliberate hits (body checking).

While not really a "sports injury," some athletes intentionally gain so much weight for sports when they are young that they set themselves up for long-term adult health problems. For example, young football linemen are encouraged to get bigger and bigger for their position, and their average size is increasing each year. According to an article in *People Magazine*, the average lineman in a top high school program these days is 232 pounds, and the average NFL lineman is nearly 30 pounds heavier than linemen were 20 years ago. This is of concern to medical experts who are aware that weight gain can lead to long-term problems such as sleep apnea, high cholesterol, early onset diabetes, heart disease, and high blood pressure.

Another "injury" or health problem is that of skin infections. Young athletes who are in wrestling, or those involved in intensive gym workouts are vulnerable because heat and moisture can create a hospitable environment for staph infections in even small skin irritations or wounds.

Finally ... if you are reluctant to let your children play a sport because of a risk of injury, you are not necessarily being over-protective—but keep risk in perspective. It is still a small risk, regardless of the scary statistics. Learn as much as you can about the real risks, and talk to other parents. Even the father of NFL great Tom Brady told Michael Silver of *Yahoo!Sports* that he "would be very hesitant to let [Brady] play today. But ... if he really wanted to play, in all likelihood I would let him." (What if Tom Brady's parents' actually had forbidden him to play football?)

STEROIDS AND SUPPLEMENT USE
(Adolescent athletes should read this section)

Steroids and performance enhancing supplements have been a big topic in professional sports over the past few years, but there is great concern that dangerous and damaging supplements and drugs are increasingly being used at the youth/teenage athletic level, as well. As mentioned previously, the use of steroids is, reportedly, the most common concern of parents of young athletes; so this is an important topic, even if you think it doesn't necessarily relate to your own child. Says Bruce Svare of the National Institute for Sports Reform, "Parents and coaches who claim there is no problem with steroids are in denial."

Note that it is not only boys who use steroids; one study actually showed that roughly a third of young steroid users were girls. In fact, a recent University of Minnesota study claims that *6% of high school and middle school boys, and 4½% of high school and middle school girls are using anabolic steroids.*

Experts in the field of substance abuse have explained that "teenagers don't have the judgment that is required for making these decisions, and that they are much more responsive to the potential short-term results than the reality of the potential long-term risks. Kids see others use the products, and they develop a false sense of security." They also complain that it is hard to convince kids that steroids are risky drugs, because they don't get "high" from them.

Of course there are nutritional supplements that are considered possibly worthwhile, and probably safe. However, experts emphasize that any use of supplements should be done with educated supervision and continued evaluation/monitoring.

Following is a brief summary of an important, true story about two young athletes' use of steroids that appeared in *Sports Illustrated Kids*. Whether or not you are concerned about your own children using steroids, it is worth the effort to have them read this, because they may know someone who is considering steroid use.

The story is about Taylor Hooton of Dallas, Texas, and one of his friends, Chris Wash—teenagers in the upscale community of Plano, Texas. Taylor dreamed of being the top varsity pitcher in high school, and Chris wanted to bulk up for his 10th grade basketball team—even though he was already on the team, at 6'2" and 180 pounds. But he also wanted to be "the toughest kid in school."

Chris started taking a type of steroid that he easily obtained from a health food store called Androstenedione ("Andro"). Though he felt angry and shaky when taking the Andro, he continued, and eventually went on to try the more serious *anabolic* steroids, which he was able to get from "a friend of a friend." While taking the anabolic steroids, Chris worked out hard and saw physical changes; however, his basketball skills didn't improve. What did change were his moods and behavior, and he was kicked off the basketball team because he often expressed significant anger.

Around the same time, Taylor Hooton also started using anabolic steroids. After several months he stopped using them, but he became very depressed—which is a side effect of steroid withdrawal. At the age of 17, Taylor Hooton committed suicide.

At the same time that Taylor committed suicide, Chris was going "on and off" steroids, and was struggling with his own depression and suicidal thoughts—but he got through that. Says Chris, "I can say this: They [steroids] messed up my life. They held me back from going to college and held me back from playing basketball. I know steroids affect everybody differently, but is it worth the risk to even try them?" In a *Newsweek* interview, Chris further lamented, "I could have had a scholarship to play ball in college. Basketball was my life. It's who I was."

After Taylor Hooton's suicide, Taylor's parents established a foundation in his name in an attempt to prevent young athletes from using steroids. The foundation provides information to educate kids, parents, and coaches about the dangers of steroid use. Sadly, there are many stories similar to Taylor's that appear on the foundation website.   (See Appendix)

TOO MUCH EMPHASIS ON WINNING

In a national PTA survey, half of the parents who responded said that if they could change one thing about youth sports, they would "want their coach to be less focused on winning."

It is quite true that some youth coaches focus too much on winning, and that can be a problem with the younger sports teams. There is so much more to teach than winning. But the problem is not just the coaches. Note in the following survey that "winning" showed up on the *parents'* list of reasons for kids to play sports. So, are (some) parents just as guilty as the coaches in their emphasis on winning? Just asking......

The New York Times published the following survey in which parents and kids (age 8-10) were separately asked to choose the three most important reasons for the child to play competitive, organized sports:

The parents' top reasons   ## The kids' top reasons

Being challenged   Having fun
Learning to compete   Learning new skills
Winning   Making friends

Much of the research done on "kids and winning" supports the notion that kids would prefer to have more playing time on a team that loses, than to sit on the bench of a team that wins. To kids ... playing is more fun than winning. ("Winning" didn't even show up on the kids' list of reasons to play sports.) As one wise 11-year-old boy told *Sports Illustrated Kids*; "I like winning a lot. But if you win and don't have fun, it's like losing."
(Note that the word "fun" didn't even find its way on to the parents' list either.)

A similar study that was done with older "elite/high level" athletes *(Martin and Dodder Study)* resulted in similar findings—"fun" was still the most important motive for participation in sports.

If your child ends up with one of those "overly concerned-about-winning coaches," you can always use it as a teaching opportunity, and work towards helping your child develop a different perspective on winning and losing. In the real world, it is unlikely that you, or any parent, is going to change the coach's attitude.

There are several organizations that are working on training and teaching coaches to adjust their approach to teaching kids about winning and losing—encouraging coaches to focus more on the process of playing, developing, practicing, and improving. (See Appendix)

TOO MUCH SPORTS ...
TOO LITTLE EVERYTHING ELSE

A major premise of this book is that participation in sports can be of great value in kids' lives. I also agree with many experts who feel that there can be significant problems when a child focuses only on sports—and nothing else. The concern is that when a child has no activities but athletic activities, he/she has too much identity with only sports, and not enough development of self-awareness. Children can also have a feeling of not fitting in to the world outside of sports. And, most significantly, there can be an unfortunate neglect of academics and a disrespect for the value of an education—particularly if a young athlete has somewhat unrealistic expectations that he/she will be playing a sport after high school (or college), and won't need a good education.

Those kids who do continue on with sports into high school are expected to make even more sacrifices than when they were younger, as the time requirements become more severe. They may miss out on social activities; they may miss out on the experience of having a part-time job; they may experience long-term physical injury; they may have limited exposure to people and activities outside of the sports world, etc.

With the likelihood low that a child's sports activities will lead to college and/or professional sports success, some believe that athletes who will never make it to the "next level," and who have no interest in doing so, are spending far too much time, energy, and money on developing skills "to the extreme"—skills that will not take them anywhere.

Los Angeles Times award-winning sportswriter Eric Sondheimer clearly understands the real world of youth sports because he has been covering high school sports in Southern California for a number of years. He often writes about the human side of the youth sports experience, and here is how he ended one particularly candid column: "So this is my advice to any parent who believes their young child could be the next big thing: Make sure they watch cartoons and the Discovery Channel, get plenty of time in unorganized games on the playground and, most important, learn how to read, write and do arithmetic before anybody starts pondering their future in sports."

I have experienced this issue, first hand, with my own sons who participated in sports throughout their youth and high school. My older son was devoted to sports participation, and ultimately focused on cross country and golf. Much of his high school time and his social life were built around those sports, and he was very content with his high level of involvement and focus. He knew very clearly that he didn't really want to spend his time or energy in any other way.

On the other hand, my younger son participated in sports up through his junior year of high school, but he came to realize that there were other things he would rather do than sports. So after his junior year he ended his sports participation, got a part-time job, spent time helping build an airplane, and filled his plentiful free-time with other activities.

As their parent, I can comfortably say they both made the correct choices ... *for them*. (I want to emphasize that they had to make the choices themselves.) My younger son learned and gained so much through having a part-time job, and he would have missed out on all of that if he had simply repeated one more year of sports activity. But my older son went on to play college golf, and his personal life continued to be built around his golf and cross country friends. They are both satisfied with their choices.

In baseball star Shane Victorino's biography, his mother talked about Shane playing baseball in Little League and through high school: "That boy was unbelievably committed. When others were going to the beach, he was going to practice or to play a game. I would even feel sorry for him because he gave up a lot of his fun time to play, but he understood the commitment."

Samantha Mewis, a US National Olympic soccer player, told *PatriotLedger.com* that she sacrificed some high school experiences because, while training for the national team, she could only play a few games with her high school team. Said Mewis, "With the high school team we're so much closer to each other. I'm missing out on good friendships, but playing with the United States team, I couldn't pass that up. With the national team, it's like a competition. At high school it's more like a family."

Carly Patterson, Olympic gold medalist in gymnastics, told *Junior Scholastic Magazine* that she has made a lot of sacrifices to accomplish what she accomplished. In fact she even admitted to her "jealousy of her younger sister's 'regular' life ... going to public school, having sleepovers with friends, eating junk food ... I can't do that because I need to rest and eat healthy," said Carly. And in describing how she was able to manage an intense practice schedule and school, she responded, "It was pretty hard ... I wouldn't even have time to make friends."

Professional soccer player Santino Quaranta started with D.C. United at the age of 16, at which time he told *Sports Illustrated* that he sometimes regretted that he didn't get to be a normal teenager—but, ultimately, he felt that it was worth it.

Finally ... the bottom line is ... while no high achievement comes without some sacrifice, each individual needs to consider whether the sacrifices are worth it *for them*.

SACRIFICES MADE BY A YOUNG ATHLETE'S FAMILY

The family of a devoted young athlete makes many sacrifices as well, and those sacrifices have to be constantly monitored for their worthiness. When a parent is driving one child to one sports practice; picking up another child from another sports practice; picking up another child from yet another sports practice, there is little time left for supervision of homework or preparation of a family meal. And when kids are practicing a sport after school, coming home for dinner, and then doing homework after dinner, there is little time for relaxed downtime. In addition, younger siblings get caught up in this rat race; they may be stuck either riding in the car all evening, or sitting passively at someone's practice.

Complicated sports schedules may mean fewer family vacations, and less time for family bonding over dinner. A *US News and World Report* article highlighted this issue with a claim made by psychiatrist Alvin Rosenfeld that "in the past 20 years, structured sports time has doubled, while family dinners have been cut by a third, and family vacations have decreased 28%."

Writing an essay in *USA Today*, youth sports expert Robert Lipsyte expressed his concerns about trends in youth sports, and he specifically refered to a book by Tom Farrey called *Game On: The All-American Race to Make Champions of Our Children*. Lipsyte wrote, "As kids grow, parents hold them back a grade so they will be heavier and more coordinated than classmates; they mortgage their houses to enroll them in tennis, golf, gymnastic academies, shove them into travel teams; and send them to private coaches, camps, psychologists, trainers, nutritionists, hoping that by age 13 they will be scouted by the pros. Families sacrifice to create winners." Lipsyte goes on to say, "No wonder a kid might be tempted to throw a crack-back block, spike a second baseman, shoot steroids or cheat on an exam to try to justify that sacrifice."

Participation in youth sports also costs a fair amount of money—not even counting the extremely expensive elite/travel teams. It can be difficult for families to afford the cost of enrollment, uniforms, and equipment for even one child, let alone more than one. Though nearly all youth sports programs do have allowances for families with financial difficulty, it is often not enough.

POOR BEHAVIOR ...
DETERIORATION IN BEHAVIOR
(It isn't just the kids ...)

A 2010 Reuters/Ipsos survey on youth sports around the world indicated that the <u>United States has the worst behaved parents at children's sporting events</u>.

There is a general consensus among those involved in youth sports that negative and aggressive behavior is increasing in an alarming way—parents toward coaches; coaches toward parents; coaches toward athletes; athletes toward coaches; community members toward teams; athletes toward parents; and every other combination that I haven't thought of. (Even the poor snack shack volunteers are subject to abuse.)

Foremost among experts' concerns is that children are learning improper sportsmanship and poor behavior from misbehaving adults—both parents and coaches. In an essay in *USA Today*, author and youth sport expert Robert Lipsyte expresses serious concern about these negative adult behaviors, emphasizing that children take the lessons they learn in sports along with them into adulthood.

Specifically, Lipsyte makes the case that young athletes are exposed to "dueling lessons." They learn the rewards of discipline, playing fair, and working hard; but at the same time they may experience the "punishment-free payoff of cheating." He goes on to stress that adults involved in youth sports must try to "avoid a win-at-all-cost mentality that has given rise to recruiting scandals, academic cheating, helmet spearing, bean balls, steroids and industrial espionage ..."

Rest assured, parents. There are organizations working to make changes in this aspect of youth sports, and there is a clear desire to see reform. (See Appendix)

UNREALISTIC EXPECTATIONS

ESTIMATED PROBABILITY OF COMPETING IN ATHLETICS BEYOND THE HIGH SCHOOL INTERSCHOLASTIC LEVEL
(NCAA RESEARCH---2013---ncaa.org)

SPORT	%High School to NCAA	% NCAA to Professional	%High School to Professional
Men's Basketball	3.3	1.2	0.03
Women's Basketball	3.7	0.9	0.03
Football	6.5	1.6	0.08
Baseball	6.8	9.4	0.07
Men's Ice Hockey	11.3	0.8	0.07
Men's Soccer	5.7	1.9	0.09

Many young athletes think—unrealistically—that they are going to at least play college sports. Many parents of young athletes think—unrealistically—that their child is going to at least play college sports. They expect to get a full scholarship and some even fully expect to go to the pros.

Why is this section included under "The Downside of Youth Sports?" The answer is: Because there are negative ramifications to those unrealistic expectations. Those expectations need to be "managed."

But what's wrong with kids and/or parents aiming for the moon and the stars when it comes to playing sports as college and professional athletes?

This is a difficult topic to discuss because there is a very fine line between "managing expectations" of an athlete and "quashing dreams and goals." Of course, no parent wants to stomp on the dreams of their children, and some kids do fulfill their dreams of an athletic future. But the facts are the facts.

Those involved in youth sports want kids and parents to most clearly understand that *no young athlete should ever ignore their academic efforts with the assumption that their sport and their ability will take care of them.* As Morgan Wootten, one of the all-time most successful high school basketball coaches, explained in *Occupational Outlook Quarterly*: "I always tell my players ... Dream your dreams, but don't let athletics use you or abuse you. You have to be prepared for the day they take the ball away. And it will happen sooner than you think."

In his book, *Spoiled Sport*, author John Underwood complains that it is difficult to get this real world message across to young people who are deluded by the glamour in professional athletics. Says Underwood, "The pro myth is fed by an irresistible hype that there is a pot of gold at the end of the rainbow. The pot is smaller than many young people think. And the rainbow fades very quickly."

A humorous depiction of unrealistic expectations was produced in a sports blog post by Rufus D. DelSantos. Mockingly taking on the tone of a well-known Nike commercial in which Michael Jordan recites the statistics of his mistakes, DelSantos wrote, "I've missed more than 9,000,000 shots trying to make it in basketball. I've skipped more than 15,000 hours worth of schooling to practice basketball. I've played and lost almost 350 basketball games, but yet signed up for more. I've never been trusted to take the game-winning shot, but I never allowed that to undermine my confidence that I was going to be a star. I've failed over and over and over again trying to make it in basketball. And that is why I now sit at age 30, in a cubicle, depressed, in a dead-end job, with no future."

Finally ... more specific guidance on this important topic is better left to sports psychologists and experts in the field: sources of information are provided in the Appendix of this book.

SO MUCH TO THINK ABOUT......

There are numerous aspects to youth sports, and so many decisions and influences along the way.

Some of those decisions will be made by the parent; most by the athlete.

The decisions certainly aren't life and death. They may just seem like it at the time.

AGE TO BEGIN PLAYING *ORGANIZED* SPORTS

According to psychologist Dr. Shane Murphy, children in the United States are starting "organized" sports at far too young an age. Wrote Murphy, on the sports website momsteam.com; "It's not so much that we have crazy parents. We have a crazy sports system. ... Many European nations don't even put kids in competitive soccer until age 13."

One of the most common misconceptions among parents about organized youth sports is that kids should start playing as soon as they can (4 to 5 years old) or they will fall behind other kids. But experts agree that this perception is incorrect. In fact, it is generally believed that the risks of a child starting sports too young tend to outweigh any benefits. This doesn't mean kids this age shouldn't have some type of physical activity, however; it is the "organized" part of it that they refer to.

What are the risks of starting "organized" sports at too young of an age? Some of those risks are discussed under the "Injuries" section of this book, but there is also a risk of burnout, loss of interest in the sport (or sports, in general), and a loss of self-esteem and self- confidence.

Michael Bergeron, a professor of exercise physiology, has been vocal about this topic, and has pointed out in public forums that there are significant differences in physical and mental development among children between the ages of 3 – 5. In fact, some children are actually not even physically capable of doing things that others the same age are able to do at these ages. The differences then create frustration, anxiety, and loss of enthusiasm for the activity.

Bergeron suggests that "any sports-like activity for these young children has to be built around fun and activity, not skill development." Bergeron also points out that, "When play becomes beset by rules such as, 'don't pick up a soccer ball, don't kick a basketball,' kids can lose their natural enthusiasm and willingness to try new things."

Note, however, that there is a key difference between the idea of playing organized sports, in general, and playing organized sports at a serious, structured level. What most experts attempt to tell parents is that it is generally fine to begin children as young as 5 or 6 in *loosely organized* sports. Most also agree that sports should not be taken very seriously with young children, in terms of pressure to win and skill development. The lessons taught to young kids should be related more to behavior, teamwork, and—most of all—how to have fun and be active. The skill development will eventually come, and kids can learn specific skills quite quickly at a later age.

In defense of parents, it must be said that most just don't know what to do because varying opinions and interests float among other parents—and they panic. Feeling that they are up against the clock, parents fear that their kids will be at a long-term disadvantage if they don't play organized sports early enough.

You still might be waiting to hear one specific age when a child should begin organized sports, but not even the experts can provide that. Much depends on the individual child, the child's physical and emotional development, and the child's interest in even participating. It also depends on the structure and attitude of any given athletic program.

There are also variables that differ with each sport. Some sports are more suited to "early specialization" than others, as highlighted in a study by Istvan Balyi and Ann Hamilton. Their study indicates that sports such as diving, figure skating, gymnastics, and table tennis require more "sport specific," specialized training, so there is an advantage to starting younger. But they report that sports such as track and field, cycling, racquet sports, combative sports, rowing, and all team sports are more suited to "later specialization," because they require, and benefit from, a more generalized approach to early training.

In particular, parents seem to be most concerned about the proper age to start kids in youth football, because of football's physically taxing nature. Again, there is no specific answer to that question; however, the Balyi/Hamilton research indicates that kids can start football at a relatively late age, just as with other team sports. There will be far less risk in waiting a year or two for your child to play football than in starting a year or two too early.

The Pop Warner football program allows for flexibility in starting age, as it is designed for kids between the ages of 5 and 16, and kids typically enter the program at any age between 5 and 13. But there are still some kids who don't even start playing football until they are in high school. Keep this in mind: *Superstar quarterback Tom Brady did not start playing football until he was 14 years old, because his father didn't think he was physically developed enough.*

Following are a few additional examples of successful athletes who did not get serious about sports/their sport until a bit of an older age:

Olympic gold medalist Michael Phelps—considered the "best competitive swimmer ever"—started swimming at 7 years old in order to learn water safety. However, he has often claimed that he didn't even like putting his face in the water at first, and that he didn't get serious about swimming until he was about 11 years old.

Jon Steller, once one of the best volleyball players on his top ranked college team, told *NCAA.com* that he didn't start playing volleyball until he was about 12 years old, and that he was the last person chosen for his 7th grade volleyball team.

NBA superstar LeBron James started playing organized sports at 9 years old—starting with PeeWee football—but didn't start playing organized basketball until he was 10 years old.

First overall 2006 NFL draft pick Mario Williams told *Sports Illustrated Kids*, "Growing up I was into baseball. I got into football in middle school. Then in high school I jumped into it a little more. Then high school to college, a little more. A lot of people think you have to start out playing football to be good at it. You don't have to. For me, it was just part of growing up and being a kid."

Cynthia Cooper-Dyke, considered to be one of the best WNBA players ever, didn't start playing organized basketball until she was 16 years old.

Former professional tennis player Taylor Dent is the son of parents who both played tennis at a high level, but he has said that his parents did not put much pressure on him to play tennis. His dad wanted him to do it on his own so he would enjoy it longer. Taylor has said that he hung out with his friends, played video games, and didn't even start playing tennis until he was about 10 or 11 years old. And it wasn't until high school that he began to take it seriously.

NFL quarterback Joe Flacco grew up with 4 brothers in a family that he has described as "sports-crazed." Though there was always a pick-up game of some sport in his neighborhood, he claims that his parents didn't allow him to play organized football until he was in 7th grade.

Lucas Giolito, first round Major League Baseball pick in 2012, says that he tried snowboarding, surfing, basketball, water polo, golf, and T-ball when he was a kid, and didn't get serious about baseball until his early teen years.

Nevertheless ... common sense implies that if a child is going to play sports growing up, he/she should probably at least be exposed to one or two sports before the age of 10. By this age, kids are beginning to discover personal interests, and they can't "discover" sports if they are not exposed to sports. Also, a study reported in *Sports Illustrated* indicates that, "If a girl doesn't participate in sports by age 10, there is only a 10% chance she will particpate at age 25." (They didn't mention boys in this study, unfortunately.)

Olympic softball star Jennie Finch is one of many exceptions, in that she did begin playing T-ball at 5 years old—starting a relatively intense immersion early on. Her parents encouraged her love of baseball, and her mom took her to Dodger games. Her dad acted as her personal coach, and practiced with her in her own batting cage in the backyard. However, Finch wasn't so wrapped up in baseball/softball that she ignored other sports; in fact, she played basketball and volleyball in high school, as well, and was captain of her basketball, volleyball, and softball teams her senior year.

CHOOSING WHICH SPORTS TO PLAY

Well-respected sports performance consultant Jeff Troesch, an expert in mental skills training and performance enhancement, offers this advice: *"Allow a child to choose whether or not to participate in a particular sport. Nothing will motivate a child more than the sense of investment that comes in choosing his/her own activities. On the other hand, little will reduce a youngster's motivation more than having a parent dictate their participation. My suggestion is that the child be compelled to participate in something positive, and that the choice of activity be his/her own."*

When children are young it is usually easy to choose what sport they will play, as communities typically emphasize one or two of the "primary" sports, depending on the season. So trying out the sport that most other kids are playing is probably the best way to go, because this approach eases kids into organized athletic activity without—hopefully—any pressure. They will be in a healthy social environment that includes other local kids, and they will be playing a sport that is somewhat familiar. Also, these sports are typically well-publicized through communities or schools, so you don't have to go looking for them. Even if you want your child to eventually try a less common sport, it is still worthwhile to try the more common sports first.

A parent's role can be to encourage a child to try different sports, and to expose the child to various athletic activities; but there is only so much a parent can, and should, do to influence the choice. The following are a few examples of this philosophy at work among the early years of some successful athletes:

Beau Hossler, a teenage golf star, was already a star baseball player when he started playing golf at the age of 8. He loved golf immediately, and eventually chose it over baseball—in spite of his stepfather's admittedly serious efforts to maintain Beau's interest in baseball. "But," says his stepfather, "it didn't work."

Barbara Hopewell, the mother of Olympic gold medalist swimmer Summer Sanders, has often described her own love for horses, and how she hoped Summer would love them too. She made a concerted effort to get Summer into this activity: she signed her up for riding lessons, frequently took her to the barn, and rode horses with her. But even though Summer "never complained about riding and she did it well," Hopewell explains that Summer also "never begged to visit the horses and spend time in the barn." She finally realized that horses were not—and never would be—Summer's passion, so she gave up on that idea. In an article on *WePlay.com,* Hopewell said, "That was an important lesson. Just because you love an activity, it doesn't mean your child will. Children need to develop their own identities."

NFL quarterback Drew Brees has told how his mother wanted him to pursue tennis, long term. Though he was an excellent tennis player as a pre-teen (ranked #3 in U-12 category), Brees quit playing competitive tennis at age 13 because it was his least favorite of the five sports he was playing.

While a child should not be pushed toward a particular sport, the parent still has the important role of making sure that a child has enough exposure to a sport to make his/her own decision. It's not unusual for kids to say they don't like something long before they have enough input to make a decision, and sometimes they begin to like a sport only after they have seen some improvement or progress in their skills.

NBA star Dwyane Wade has said that he didn't like basketball at first—he preferred baseball and football. However, after his father took him to a basketball court for a week straight, Wade says he "fell in love with the game." And former NBA star Allen Iverson has said that he wasn't interested in playing basketball as a kid, because he "thought it was soft." Football was his "first love." But his mother made him go to basketball tryouts, and, as a result, he has since admitted, "I'll thank her forever"—because he came back from basketball tryouts saying, "I like basketball, too."

The trick for parents, then, is knowing when to expose, when to encourage and support, and when to back off. Expose kids to a wide variety of sports, and see "what floats their boat." Some sports will rise to the surface and some will sink.

TEAM SPORTS *vs.* INDIVIDUAL SPORTS

There are *HUGE* differences between the dynamics of individual sports and team sports. Neither format is better than the other; they are just different—very different.

Over the years I have observed that individual sports tend to attract a different type of child than do team sports. (That's a generalization, but ...) Therefore, if a child tries more than one *team* sport and has the same objections to each, switching from team sports to individual sports is certainly something to consider—before quitting sports altogether. He/she may not like the organizational structure and dynamics of a team. Some kids need direction—others are self-starters. Some kids get motivated when others pump them up—others might be more "internal" and prefer the challenge of competing against themselves.

TEAM SPORTS

The NFL's Colin Kaepernick once said; "You know what I love most about this game? Being around my teammates ... because there is no other sport where you rely on your teammates so much. The fact that you can go out there and trust ten other people without even looking at them, that's amazing."

Most adults have been on a team at one time or another and already understand many of the benefits of team sports, such as socialization, learning to take direction, learning the meaning of teamwork, the sheer fun of team synergy, etc. Team sports teach critical life skills that can serve kids throughout their lives; and teams can be supportive and build self-confidence, while providing a shared joy that many kids love. Teams also offer opportunities for shared responsibility—a chance to be "a part of something."

Team sports are also social in the mere fact that they involve large groups. And many kids consider the social aspect of a team to be just as important as the athletic aspect. Groups of athletes can have a lot of fun, and they end up spending so much time together that they develop a close bond in their function as a solid team.

But the "benefits" of team sports work both ways. When a young athlete's performance results in a dis- appointed or negative response from the team and/or parents, some kids can be overwhelmed or heartbroken. For example, former major league baseball player Todd Zeile told the *Westlake/Malibu Lifestyles* magazine that "baseball has a lot of failure in it—the best hitters in the major leagues 'fail' 7 out of 10 times at bat." Some kids can handle that dynamic and some kids can't.

INDIVIDUAL SPORTS

The late Payton Jordan, legendary college and Olympic track coach, once described the nature of running competition in this profound way: "You put on those running shorts and toe the line. You look down the track, alone in your lane. There's nobody that can substitute for you, no one to give you more courage.

There's just the tape and the stopwatch. No excuses. No second chances." (Reported in the Santa Barbara Independence newspaper.)

One significant aspect of individual sports such as golf, tennis, wrestling, track and field or cross country is that the individual athlete is in *total control* of the effect of his/her performance, and he/she is the only one who can accept either the blame or the accolades. It takes a certain amount of inner strength and confidence to accept this type of responsibility at a young age, but there are some kids who thrive on this individual accountability, responsibility, and competition; there are others who collapse.

Individual athletes tend to feel that they are really only competing with themselves, even though they are in competition with others. As Johnathan Cabral explained, after setting records in the hurdles his senior year of high school; "Every time, I go out to improve and to beat myself. The hardest thing in track is beating yourself; it's not beating the competition."

Although young athletes are competing as individuals, there is still a social environment within these sports, and there can be a very supportive team spirit in track and field, golf, wrestling, tennis, etc. There is a respect for each other that develops. And because the social pressures are much less intense, a child with a bit of a "unique" social personality can still fit in. In individual sports, children can be who they want to be, and they can be as social (or anti-social) as they want to be.

There are fewer winners and more losers, per se, in individual sports than there are in team sports—only one winner in a golf tournament, one winner in a race, one winner in a tennis match, etc. Whereas, in team competitions, only half of the athletes will lose—and half will win. This is an important consideration because some kids are better at handling "losing" than others: or, stated another way ... some kids need to "win" more than others.

Likewise, there might be fewer kudos and pats on the back for the individual athlete than there are for team athletes; and some kids are good with that, while some kids are not.

ONE SPORT SPECIALIZATION *vs.* MULTIPLE SPORTS

Baseball superstar Derek Jeter also played basketball in high school.

NFL quarterback Drew Brees lettered in baseball and football in high school, and also played basketball, soccer and tennis when he was younger.

Major League pitcher and two-time Cy Young Award winner Tim Lincecum played football, basketball, and baseball in high school.

NFL star Troy Polamalu played football, baseball, and basketball in high school.

Olympic softball star Jennie Finch lettered in softball, basketball, and volleyball in high school.

Zach Lee, 2010 MLB first round draft pick, played football and baseball in high school.

Heisman Trophy winner and #2 overall NFL draft pick in 2012, Robert Griffin III, was also a high school track star, and participated in the 2008 Olympic trials—running the 400 meter hurdles.

Baseball power hitter Giancarlo Stanton played baseball, basketball, and football in high school. (Scouts say his power comes from lower body leverage developed through football and basketball.)

The NFL's 2012 Defensive Player of the Year, J.J. Watt, lettered in baseball, basketball, and track in high school, and was the Wisconsin state champion in shot put. (He also played hockey for 10 years.)

NBA player Chase Budinger starred in basketball and volleyball in high school, and credits volleyball with helping him with his timing and anticipation in basketball.

Archie Bradley, baseball's 7th overall draft pick in 2011, was also considered one of the country's best quarterback prospects coming out of high school.

Byron Buxton was taken #2 overall in the 2012 MLB draft, but his coach told *SportsIllustrated.com* that Buxton could have been a Division I football prospect if he had wanted that. (Buxton also played high school basketball for 2 years.)

Major League Baseball's Bubba Starling played baseball, basketball, and football in high school, and initially planned to play baseball and football in college—until he was drafted 5th overall in the 2011 draft.

One of the more controversial issues today in youth sports is the question of whether young athletes should specialize in one sport year-round, or play multiple sports. The more recent trend has been for kids to focus on only one sport at younger and younger ages, and many youth coaches (and others) argue that "things are different today and kids have to specialize." As a result, some youth and high school coaches schedule off-season practices, and they show bias against multi-sport athletes. And some travel team coaches insist on a one- sport focus, as well.

Sometimes it is over-zealous parents who push their kids to specialize in only one sport in order to get a college scholarship; they have the misguided notion that an athlete MUST focus on only one sport in order to excel.

Not surprisingly, parents and athletes are confused about which approach to take, and many probably feel that they have little say in the matter. Therefore, it is noteworthy that, through the extensive research done for this book, I have observed that a backlash is developing against early specialization. In particular, child development experts and sports psychologists are speaking out to challenge this trend and are encouraging multi-sport participation into the later teen years.

Adding support to this argument is the fact that many of today's most successful college and professional athletes played multiple sports all through high school—and some were even offered scholarships for more than one sport.

There are some athletes who have even been able to play more than one sport at the college level, such as Arizona State football and baseball recruit Brandon Magee. Also, the NFL's Tony Gonzalez lettered in football, basketball, and baseball in high school, and played both football and basketball in college. (Gonzalez has often talked about how he has used his basketball skills to perfect his football performance.) In addition, NFL wide receiver Santana Moss went to the University of Miami on a track scholarship, and received a football scholarship only after walking on to the team. He continued with track, as well, and was named Most Outstanding Field Performer.

During a 2011 broadcast of a big high school football game on *Fox Sports West*, sportscasters Chris McGee and John Jackson announced an online poll that was being conducted during the game, in which viewers were asked to answer the question: *What is more beneficial for young athletes: specialization in one sport year-round or participating in multiple sports?*

Even before the results were known, Jackson (a former USC All-American) said he thought "multiple sports" was the correct answer, explaining, "A lot of people would disagree with that because the trend of high school sports these days is to specialize in one sport. But if you do have the multiple sports, that does create a balance. Having multiple sports ... it allows you to develop different muscle groups and gives your body a rest."

The results of the poll were: *45% of responding viewers answered "specialization" and 55% answered "multiple sports."* After the results were announced, Jackson laughed and said, "I think that "specialization" vote of 45% was every high school coach that was voting tonight."

Experts are quick to point out that there are tremendous advantages to playing multiple sports, such as ....

> ... a greater range of skill and muscle development from working different parts of the body.
>
> ... a reduced risk of overuse injury.
>
> ... an enhanced ability in one type of sport through the skills learned through another type of sport.
>
> ... exposure to a wider range of people.
>
> ... development of an understanding of different sports to take into adulthood—as an athlete or a fan.

... prolonging a potential college/professional athletic career.

... prevention of burnout and boredom with one sport.

Brian Grasso is another of the many voices preaching the multi-sport approach for kids. Mr. Grasso is founder of the International Youth Conditioning Association (IYCA), and is also a world renowned athletic development professional who has authored countless books, and has trained over 20,000 young athletes around the world. Grasso says, "What a growing and maturing body needs in order to remain injury free and develop optimal athletic skill is variety. The strongest and fastest athletes in any sport are the ones who had the greatest diversity of training while they were young."

Discussing specialization at a young age, respected sports nutritionist Dave Ellis told the *Daily Spark*, "People who specialize in cognitive and physical development have seen too much burnout and we now have large pools of athletes that yield very mediocre potential instead of high-end talent. There is more evidence that the athlete who didn't specialize early and was a little later in maturation might end up being the better athlete."

In an online article titled "How to Develop Your Young Athlete into a Champion Wrestler," writer Michael Fry listed STEP ONE: "Start playing football, basketball, soccer or any sport but wrestling." Fry went on to explain that he had conducted many interviews with top Eastern European wrestlers who told him that much of their training and conditioning came from playing games and participating in sports other than wrestling. He also pointed out that, although Eastern European countries and China might start kids in athletics as young as 5 years old, the children are not playing one particular sport—they are learning about movement, balance coordination and flexibility.

Along those same lines, former tennis professional Ivan Lendl has said that many Czechoslovakian hockey players take up tennis in the summer off-season to improve their conditioning and footwork. (In reverse, NFL quarterback Drew Brees credits his years of youth tennis for developing the quick footwork that he is known for in his quarterback position.)

The following are a few more examples of real-world successful athletes' experiences playing multiple sports:

A recent multi-sport athlete is Max Browne, the 2013 Gatorade National Athlete of the Year, and reportedly "the best quarterback recruit of his class." Browne played baseball, basketball, and football throughout his youth, and played basketball and football throughout high school. When asked in an interview at the Gatorade Awards how he felt about "specialization" in youth sports, he had this to say: "I encourage guys to play it all. You never know what will happen. You might fall in love with one sport one day and a different sport the next. Play it all and see what you love."

MLB star Shane Victorino not only beat the odds of "getting noticed in rural Hawaii," but he was offered scholarships in both football and baseball. On top of that, he was the Hawaii state high school track and field champion in sprints—an athletic skill that has served him well on the field. (Fans call him "The Flyin' Hawaiian.")

Candis Kapuscinksi won the *HighSchoolSports.net* Ultimate Athlete Award in 2011, having been MVP on her high school basketball, soccer and softball teams. Said a spokesman for that *USA Today* award: "The panel of judges thought that Candis's excellence in multiple sports truly defined what we were looking for in an Ultimate Athlete."

NFL quarterback Colin Kaepernick played football, basketball, and baseball in high school, and was nominated for All-State his senior year in all three sports. Though he particularly stood out in baseball, and received several scholarship offers as a baseball pitcher, he has said that he desperately wanted to play college football, not baseball. However, he didn't get much college attention for football his senior year of high school and only received one scholarship offer (Nevada).

As told by Andrea Adelson of *ESPN.com*, the University of Nevada was still looking for a quarterback in December of Kaepernick's senior year, and they had heard a little about Kaepernick; so Nevada's assistant *football* coach, Barry Sacks, went to see him play *basketball*—since it was too late to see him play football. Sacks ended up recruiting Kaepernick for the Nevada football team, even though he never got a chance to evaluate his football skills. Explained Sacks, "It's [basketball] one of the tools you can use to evaluate an athlete. You can see not only his athleticism, but his competitiveness and his toughness."

In an article from *ResponsibleSports.com*, several professional athletes were asked about their youth sports experiences, and how they feel about kids playing multiple sports. Following are a few of their comments, taken from the article:

Jessica Mendoza, Olympic Gold Medal winning softball player: "I was a two-sport athlete in high school (basketball and softball), and I would say a majority of my USA teammates were two-sport, if not three-sport athletes, as well. No doubt about it, definitely play as many sports as you can."

Doug Wilson, Hall of Fame hockey player and pro hockey General Manager: "The best thing that my parents ever did ... they gave me the opportunity to play everything. I was a pretty good hockey player, but I wasn't really good in maybe one of the other sports. They'd make me go play that sport so that I would have the perspective from the other kids that might not be really good at something, but they're playing it because they love it."

Alexi Lalas, USA World Cup soccer player: "I was heavily involved in ice hockey. And I tried absolutely everything out there."

Jessica Colby, a US Olympic team member in the sport of hammer throw, has said that the Olympics was her dream as a runner in a youth track program at 8 years old: she only tried the shot put because the track program gave a medal for trying every sport at least once. Colby ended up setting a conference record with the shot put, and decided that would be "her sport," after all. (She also played basketball and ran sprints in high school.)

The youth track and field programs I was involved in do "bribe" the kids this way—offering a medal at the end of the season if each event is tried at least once. It's remarkable how many kids are influenced by this approach and end up regularly competing in—and enjoying—events they would NEVER have tried, otherwise.

Matt Cassel, now in the NFL, went to USC on a football scholarship, but his playing time was limited because he was a back-up quarterback to stars Carson Palmer and Matt Leinart. Having played high school baseball, as well, Cassel had other options; so he tried out for the USC baseball team, played on the team, and was ultimately drafted by the pros in both baseball and football.

The NFL's Antonio Gates played football and basketball in high school, but didn't even play football in college because he wasn't allowed to play two sports. So he chose to play college basketball. However, in spite of an impressive college basketball performance, NBA scouts thought he was too small for the NBA, so Gates ended up signing to play football (undrafted) and has since had a successful football career.

Professional golfer Gary Woodland played basketball and golf in high school, and golf was his favorite sport. But he only received one Division I offer to play golf, and had several offers to play basketball, so he pursued college basketball instead. But after his freshman year playing basketball at Washburn University, he changed his mind and moved to the University of Kansas to play golf—he eventually becoming one of the best golfers in the history of Kansas men's golf. He now plays the PGA Tour.

NBA superstar LeBron James has often spoken of his love for football, and even threatened (sort of) to switch to football during the NBA strike. He also admitted to *Sports Illustrated Kids* that he "likes football more than basketball."

Considering those who played multiple sports in high school, and had the option of playing more than one sport in college, there is probably no more dramatic example than that of Major

League Baseball star Joe Mauer—who was the only high school athlete ever to be selected as the *USA Today* High School Player of the Year in two sports. He also received numerous other sports awards his senior year. Turning down a scholarship to be quarterback at Florida State, he entered the MLB draft, and was the first overall pick in 2001. (Mauer actually played three sports in high school—football, basketball and baseball.)

This list could go on and on, but it will stop with one of the more unusual sport combinations for a multi-sport athlete: 1982 Heisman Trophy winner Herschel Walker competed in the 1992 Winter Olympics with Team USA ... in the bobsled competition.

Finally ... Tim Livingston of *ThePostGame.com* wrote an article arguing that NFL teams should try to recruit basketball players to be receivers because of their height, their hands, and vertical leap. In particular, he explained that there might be significant potential for former, or current basketball players who aren't playing in the NBA, to make the switch to the NFL—listing a few players who have done so, such as Antonio Gates, Tony Gonzalez, Darren Fells.

Livingston also got former quarterback, and current ESPN analyst, Ron Jaworski's take on the idea: "There's no question and I think clearly you're on to something," commented Jaworski. "The NFL is now a red zone game. You got to find a way to be creative in that part of the field and score touchdowns." So Livingston suggests that it is only a matter of time before his idea catches on, because "as space shrinks in the red zone, teams can gain a profound advantage by increasing their height."

NOTE: There is a common perception among young and old sports enthusiasts that these athletes who are able to play more than one sport well are just "naturally talented," so they can *naturally* do any sport well. But the research, and the real-world experiences of successful athletes do not necessarily support that perception. Rather, the research indicates that great athletes are often good at more than one sport because they bring the same work ethic and competitive spirit to each sport. And, more importantly, they bring the skills from one sport to another, enhancing their play of each of their sports. Nevertheless, the whole "talent vs. hard work" argument will always be debated, and is addressed more thoroughly in an upcoming chapter.

TRAVEL/CLUB/ ELITE/SELECT SPORTS TEAMS

Travel sports teams (also called *Elite* teams, *Club* teams, *Select* teams) are one of the controversial topics in youth sports today, and there are strong opinions on both sides of the issue. These teams have evolved over the past couple decades, but the basic premise of them is to take the best players in a sport from a general community and form teams that will travel to other towns to compete against the best players in that community. The teams generally provide a higher level of competition, a higher level of coaching, a well-connected network into the college recruiting world, and a social experience for the athletes and their families.

It is worth noting that sports experts generally believe that too many kids are participating in travel teams these days, which is having a dilution effect on the level of play in the overall system. In other words, the teams are not as "elite" as they once were.

Travel teams are sometimes coached by volunteers, but are often coached and "owned" by paid coaches. Participants must pay to be on one of these teams, and through the years these teams have taken on more of a "business profile."

One key issue with the topic of travel teams is that both parents and older kids tend to think that athletes involved in team sports *must* play on these elite teams in order to play the sport in high school, and/or to get noticed by colleges. This perception puts tremendous pressure on both the athletes and parents. But it is difficult for anyone to really know how important participation on these teams is, or is not, in terms of athletic skill development, athletic potential, college sports opportunities, the athlete's happiness, etc. Therefore, many give in to the pressure and are influenced to climb on board

It has been reported that there is a greater and greater level of conflict between some of these travel teams and the local high school teams, with some travel teams going so far as to prevent their athletes from playing their sport in high school—at all. This development is of great concern to high school coaches (of course), school administrators, and parents, who generally all agree that the athletic and social aspects of high school sports participation are far too important to dismiss.

Many experts claim that athletes don't necessarily have to play on travel teams to get noticed by colleges if they are playing on their high school teams. Particularly in today's world, where nothing evades the internet, it is said that an exceptional athlete will be found—no matter where he/she is. As one high school coach said in an article in the *Los Angeles Times*: "Our kids get seen, whether it's in practice with college coaches coming by or the tournaments we play in over the year." Nevertheless, travel/elite teams can be helpful in getting an athlete noticed if he/she is from a small, athletically low-key school.

Even if athletes do eventually play on travel teams, they don't have to start at a young age. For example, NBA star Anthony Davis didn't play travel basketball until the spring of his junior year in high school, and he only joined the AAU team because his high school was a low-profile school that didn't get much media attention. Though he and his parents were concerned about Anthony getting noticed by colleges, they were reassured by a friend, who was also a coach, that Anthony would get enough attention on that AAU team during that last year of school. Said their friend, "If you're good enough, they'll find you wherever you are."

Concerns that critics have with these travel teams is the real potential for athlete burnout and overuse injuries. There is just too much mental and physical focus on one sport. As sportswriter Ben Bolch pointed out in an article about travel basketball teams, "Some high school coaches complain that kids are burned out on basketball by September, and others have developed bad habits and poor fundamentals by playing a different style of basketball on travel teams." And, in the same article, UCLA basketball coach Ben Howland talked about the intense summer schedule in travel basketball, saying, "What I see as the biggest fallout from kids playing so many games is you're seeing kids more and more showing up to college with things like tendonitis already going on in their body. That's a worry."

Noteworthy is a segment from the website *About.com* in which the "Pros and Cons of Travel Teams" were discussed. The following are a few of the comments posted:

"My daughter played "select" ball for 8 years. She made great friends and she learned sportsmanship, built a lot of character and ultimately, learned how to be a better player." The writer went on to say, "What she never learned to deal with were the coaches. She did have some great coaches, but she also had some coaches who had no business dealing with kids. You have a 50/50 chance of getting either."

Another response: "All the playing I did (in travel teams) provided more opportunity for injury and, in the end, due to a bum shoulder, prevented me from playing in college—which is the reason I was playing so much in the first place. Also, the cost was high, and it took weekends away from being with friends and studying. But it kept me out of trouble and I got to travel."

From a former Division I athlete: "Such an over-emphasis on a child's ability in one singular facet of life severely limits the development and well-roundedness of experiences and abilities. And select sports are a severe tax on time, money, family, weekends, schoolwork, and other opportunities. A bad investment.............."

And another: "Our daughter played select basketball for several years, and while we mostly enjoyed it, we found it dismaying how important the experience was to the parents. Many of the girls had given up on sports by their sophomore or junior years, and not one girl ended up with a basketball scholarship."

A final response: "I have played select softball, basketball, and volleyball. One thing I can say for all these experiences is that they were worth it. I made friends/memories that will never leave me. But I personally believe that you must be careful at what age you start playing year-round sports, and the personality of the organization. My opinion is to wait until high school to jump in whole-heartedly."

So ... regarding whether a young athlete should join a travel team or not ... there is little more to say. Like most other parent/athlete decisions, it is an individual decision. Bottom line is that there are pros and cons to travel teams, and they might be worthwhile and appropriate for some athletes. There does seem to be a common theme, however—that athletes don't need to participate on these teams at a young age.

CHOOSING A POSITION IN A SPORT

Former NFL wide receiver Hines Ward told Sports Illustrated Kids: "Playing a lot of different positions in college helped me understand the game. For me, it gave me an edge, especially because there were more talented guys out there. It gave me a little edge that I can appreciate now."

Athletes, coaches, (and parents) might single out one position or role in a sport for any given child, thinking that focusing on one position is the best way to excel in that sport. But most of those in the know agree that it is very important that both younger and older athletes be open and willing to play different positions in their sports in order to develop the versatility and the multiple skills that higher levels of sports will require of them.

As athletes go through their youth sports career (and beyond), it is very possible that they will be required to play in positions they didn't expect to play in, and many unfamiliar roles might be thrust at them. They have to be completely open, willing, and prepared for these change-ups. It is the flexible athletes who excel, who get noticed, and who are identified as respected "team players." Athletes with a broad base of skills will have more options and opportunities long- term.

Anthony Davis, the top NBA draft pick in 2012, was given only mild attention by college recruiters while in high school. But the summer before his senior year he had an 8" growth spurt that moved him into shot blocking and rebounding roles on his basketball team. Having only played a perimeter game until then, he felt challenged because he had to change his game very quickly, and had to develop the new skills that were required of him. Said Davis, "Some of the shots I didn't know how to do. Some of the things I'd never heard of because I used to play on the perimeter." Nevertheless, said his father, "He knows the language of basketball. He listens well and catches on quick." And Davis credits his additional skill development for finally attracting college attention.

There may be a position that an athlete likes to play more than any other position, but that doesn't mean that position is the most appropriate one. There may be a position that the athlete's skills, size, etc. seems best suited for by traditional standards, but a particular team might not go by "traditional standards." And, while athletes might feel they know better than anyone which position they should play, they might be right, or they might be wrong. Also, there are always new trends in training, in strategy, in equipment, in game-plans, etc., and the role of various positions can change with the trends.

The following opinions and experiences of successful athletes emphasize the previous points: (Parents, maybe you can use some of these stories in making this point to your kids ... and their coaches.)

Gatorade California Girls Soccer Player of the Year for 2009-2010, Abby Dahlkemper, was on the U17 National Soccer team, and was recruited by many Division I college soccer programs. Though she primarily played offense in high school, she was recruited as a defender by her chosen school, UCLA. As she told *The Daily Journal*, "... I think it [having played offense] helps me understand the forwards and what they're thinking when they're attacking. I was willing to play any position that can help the team do well. If it's attacking, I'll attack. If it's defending, I'll defend."

Though NFL player Denard Robinson was a star starting quarterback at Michigan, he also trained to play running back, wide receiver, and both kick and punt returner. For that reason he was viewed as a "multi-faceted talent," according to a *Yahoo!Sports* profile, and that position flexibility attracted the attention of NFL scouts. In fact, in his senior year he was the only player from his Michigan team to be invited to participate in the NFL combine (as a wide receiver), and was drafted in the fifth round of the 2013 draft.

Yankees first baseman Mark Teixeira told *Sports Illustrated Kids* that he mostly played short stop in Little League, and he also pitched a little.

The #1 NFL draft pick in 2013, Eric Fisher, played at Central Michigan and, by most accounts, he wasn't the classic superstar to end up as the top pick. But it was his versatility in playing multiple positions while he was in college that made him all the more attractive to the NFL, say several sports pundits.

Byron Buxton, the top high school baseball player in 2012, and taken #2 in the MLB draft, was a starting pitcher and a center fielder in high school. Described often as a "five tool athlete" (skilled at hitting, power, running, throwing, fielding), with the potential to be a great pitcher, he is reportedly not interested in pitching and prefers the outfield, where he now plays—a position that helped him win a number of awards in 2013. (Buxton also played quarterback, wide receiver, and defensive back for his high school football team.)

Professional soccer goalie Terry Boss played soccer in the central defender position throughout his youth, and almost all of high school, but he switched over to playing in the goal during his senior year. Explained Boss in an *Eastbay.com* blog post: "I just remember being in the goal and knowing it was something I was supposed to be doing. It just felt so natural that it took off and I played my senior season in the goal and some doors opened to go to college."

Dallas Clark, considered to be one of the best tight ends in the NFL, walked on at Iowa as a linebacker and thought that was where he belonged. But he didn't perform so well in that position, so his coach talked him into trying the tight end position. (Clark says it took him a year to decide to make the change.) Referring to that change, his coach said in an interview with the *Iowa Gazette:* "Sometimes the abilities players have don't always translate when they are in the wrong position, and clearly we had him in the wrong spot."

Colt Lyerla, a University of Oregon tight end, was dominant on both offense and defense in high school, playing running back, wide receiver, and linebacker. (His nickname was "Mr. Versatility.") As a result, he received more than 30 college scholarship offers. But even after accepting an offer from Oregon, he admitted that he wasn't sure which position he would play, telling *Sports Illustrated,* "I have to see how I fit in their system. It's just gonna depend on how far back I'd be on the depth chart." In the same interview Lyerla also explained that his "experience in multiple roles helps him anticipate plays before they unfold."

In a *USA Today* interview by Greg Boeck, current NBA player Chase Budinger's transition to a new position in his first year at

Arizona was described as difficult. Said one college coach, "He [Budinger] gets lost defensively, but that will come over time. He knows the game." And, said Budinger, himself, "I'm still catching on. It's a tough transition," admitting that he "mostly stood around" on defense in high school."

Though former #1 MLB draft pick Bryce Harper predominantly, and very successfully, played catcher in his stellar high school and college baseball career, the Nationals drafted him as an outfielder in order to extend his career, and to get him into the major leagues sooner.

Albert Pujols has played every position except pitcher, catcher, and center field in his Major League career.

There always have to be exceptions ... and one of the more famous exceptions to "remaining flexible about a playing position" is the story of former NFL star Jim Plunkett, who was a stand-out high school quarterback and went to Stanford also as a quarterback. But he had health issues and ended up having a less-than-impressive freshman year. As a result, Plunkett was asked to switch to defensive end—but he refused to, and threatened to transfer. He remained the Stanford quarterback ... and won the Heisman Trophy his senior year.

THE LESS POPULAR POSITIONS AND SKILLS

When "Sports Illustrated Kids" posed the question: Why did you become a pitcher? to MLB's Dontrelle Willis, his answer was, "Nobody else on my team wanted to pitch, to be totally honest. I figured it was a good way to get on the field."

There is tremendous opportunity for young athletes to develop themselves for positions in a sport that are less popular than others. They can find a niche and "make it their own."

THE BASKETBALL CENTER

The center position in basketball is said to be the one that most kids (and adults) try to avoid. Said retired player Nate McMillan to *ThePostGame.com*: "We're looking for them [centers]. You want them, just where are they?" And, as Kevin Fixler wrote in his "The Daily Fix" column: "The belief in the importance of centers and the shortage of prospects makes them high in demand." Fixler also quotes basketball training consultant Clifford Ray as saying, "I just hope that another couple of great centers come down the pike so that it will enhance more of the young people to want to be centers. Not to try to avoid playing center, but to want to play the position and really learn the position."

Dwight Howard told *ThePostGame.com*, "[Center] is a very tough position. It's one that a lot of people really don't want to play, because of how physical and tough it is. You have to be the tough guy on the court." He even admitted, "I always wanted to be a point guard, but then I started to grow, so I played center once I got to the league." (Howard was a power forward all through high school.) Even legendary center Kareem Abdul Jabbar has admitted that he always wanted to be a forward ... but he grew.

THE PUNTER, THE KICKER, AND THE SNAPPER

According to a *Sports Illustrated* article, most college football programs in past years tried to get by without allocating scholarships for special teams players; but that has changed, and more and more of these positions are being filled with scholarship athletes. As estimated by kicking coach Jamie Kohl, "... 50–60 kickers, punters, and even long-snappers earn FBS scholarships in a given year."

The punting position is generally considered a less- than-exciting spot, and is often one that players "end up playing" as they give way to the competition in their favored position. However, according to a *Los Angeles Times* article, the position is taking on more prominence as NFL scouts are specifically recruiting for it—particularly in Australia, where kids grow up kicking in football because they are not allowed to throw the ball. As a result, Australian kids are now training to punt in the American style—trying to get a scholarship to an American university.

After exhibiting punting skills in high school, Brad Wing was offered a scholarship to Louisiana State, and quickly became somewhat of a celebrity due to both a 73-yard punt and a fake punt that ended up as popular videos on YouTube. And in 2012, Bryan Anger was the first punter in 17 years to be taken in the "first 75" of the NFL draft.

According to *Sports Illustrated*, the kicker in college football is becoming more of a game-changing/game-winning position than in the past, and the kicks "mean a lot more." As explained by former kicker, and current kicking coach Jamie Kohl, "The games are tight because of scholarship limits and other factors, and a lot of times it comes down to precious kicks." At the same time, the kickers in college football are considered better than they have ever been, even though some of their "misses" have been so prominent.

Kickers' skills are also much more refined than some may think. As explained by college kicker Quinn Sharp, "People are like, 'Aw, you just get up there and kick it, but it's not like that. It's a lot more technical than people think it is. If you're off by a couple inches, it's not going to go through." But the mental aspect of kicking and handling the pressure of the position is "easily more than half of it," according to former Nebraska kicker Brett Maher. "If you're not mentally strong and sharp, I don't think it matters how far you can kick it."

The *Sports Illustrated* article also pointed out that many kickers are walk-ons, and they sometimes even beat the scholarship kickers for a spot on the team.

Tanner Gibas, an excellent high school long snapper, accepted a four-year scholarship to the University of Kansas, but admitted to the *Los Angeles Times*, "I was never into sports. I never liked football. I played Gremlin flag football and didn't like it at all. My dad said 'try one more time.' I never thought I'd be playing college football. It's very weird." (Tanner's older brother also had a college scholarship as a long snapper.) Referring to the long snapper position, Gibas was quoted in the *Times* article as saying, "I recommend it to kids who aren't very good in football. Anyone can snap the football. It's all technique ... but long snappers are getting better and better." (Gibas gave up football in college for medical reasons.)

Another long snapper, Jon Dorenbos, has told of his dreams to play football at a Division I school after playing linebacker at a community college for two years—but he received no offers. Then he heard about a need for a long snapper at the University of Texas El Paso and he earned that spot using his limited experience as a long snapper in high school. Dorenbos wasn't drafted into the NFL out of college, but he signed as a free agent, and played in the NFL as a long snapper until a knee injury sidelined him.

THE BACK-UP (IN ANY POSITION)

Back-up players just never know if their time will come, but it is not unheard of for 3rd string players to jump into a game and shine. Some back-ups get frustrated and move on to different schools/teams, some wait for their chance and get it, and others get lost in the disappointment and frustration of the back-up life—and just quit.

In a *USA Today* article, Jim Sorgi described what it was like playing back-up quarterback to Peyton Manning in the 2007 Super Bowl. He said, "It's a great job and it's a bad job. I'm the guy nobody wants to see play. My job is not a lot of pressure all day, every game. But when the moment comes there's going to be a lot of pressure." In the same article, former quarterback

Rodney Peete described Sorgi's back-up quarterback opportunity as, "He's getting to go to school from one of the greatest quarterbacks of all time. It's an invaluable experience that will pay off later."

Former Super Bowl back-up quarterback Brian Griese described the position in this way; "It's not easy. It's like when you were in the 10th grade, and you studied really hard for a test, and you're ready for the test. You go to take it and they tell you you're not going to take it that day."

THE UTILITY PLAYER IN BASEBALL

Los Angeles Times writer Andrew Owens wrote about the value of the "utility player" in professional baseball, another position that some consider under-appreciated. In profiling MLB utility player Jerry Hairston, Jr., Owens explained that the versatility of a utility player provides injury insurance for several positions, and can prolong a career. Explained Hairston, himself; "It's helped me prolong my career, for sure. When a guy goes down, I can play shortstop every day for a while, I can play third base every day for a while, center field, wherever. That's definitely helped me."

Owens also wrote that the utility player's versatility can even provide an entry point into the pros that might not be attainable playing only one position. Describing Elian Herrera as a player who earned a big league chance, in part because he is versatile, Owens quotes Dodgers Manager Don Mattingly as saying, "You may not play well enough at one position to say, 'This guy's a big league third baseman.' You need role players like that. Being able to play all those positions helped get him [Herrera] to the big leagues."

TREND FOR YOUNGER "RECRUITS" AND "SUPERSTAR" PROCLAMATIONS

As discussed on Rivals.com, in an article by writer Steve Megargee, athletic recruiting is happening extremely early now because "everyone is doing it"; but the college coaches don't necessarily all like the trend. "The offers [to very young athletes] are being made on potential, not performance," says Megargee. Quoting the Clemson football coach in the article: "I don't like it, but there's nothing I can do about it. I'm hesitant to offer guys in the 10th grade. There are certain guys who can qualify for that, but not many. It makes it tough ... they've still got some maturing to do as a person. They've got to have a couple more years of good decision making and production as a player. It's definitely a new era we're in, but it's where we are."

There are more stories than ever about really young kids receiving offers for college scholarships, and these young athletes are given an undue amount of attention—but are too immature to handle it. At the same time, the internet has become another source of pressure on young athletes who stand out, because social networking sites and recruiting-related sites can make the kids even more vulnerable to criticism, jealousy, harassment, contact/communication, etc.

In this current atmosphere, the stress created by the adulation and attention heaped on these young athletes is only beginning to be understood, but child development experts and sports psychologists are expressing concern—while the NCAA has attempted to address these concerns. Under emergency legislation, the NCAA voted to classify 7th and 8th graders officially as "prospects" in men's basketball so that the they can control elite camps and clinics set up by college coaches who are trying to gain an early advantage in the recruiting process. But, according to some, this plan has backfired, in that it is making the athletes even more openly exposed to college recruiting.

In another attempt to control recruiting for football, the NCAA tried to delay the recruiting process by passing legislation in 2010 that prevented colleges from making written offers to prospects before August 1, at the start of their senior years. (The previous date had been September 1 before the junior year.) However, because there are no limits on verbal offers, coaches simply take advantage of that loophole.

Some defend the practice of giving attention to younger kids by saying that these early promises are basically "empty" anyway, because "anything can happen" to the athlete, the offer, or the coach. However, others don't agree, explaining that stress from the pressure, expectations, undue attention, and potential unkept promises can destroy the psyche of a young, developing athlete. "Where is the benefit?" they ask.

The harm of showering attention and opportunities on young athletes is evident through the short history of "former soccer star" Freddy Adu. He made headlines at the age of 13 when he signed a one million dollar endorsement deal with Nike and was given a Major League Soccer contract at the age of 14.

At that time there were unusually high expectations placed on the shoulders of this young teenager, and there was tremendous pressure on him. But Adu did not live up to expectations, and ended up bouncing around soccer teams in Europe and the US; now, his future in soccer remains uncertain—and he is only in his early twenties.

According to a *Yahoo!Sports* article, everyone around Adu considered him "self-centered," and complained that his style of play was one that "dictates that he be the star, the central piece or nothing at all." Though he had skills, he was lacking mental maturity. (An aside, in Adu's defense: *Can Adu really be faulted for that? He was so young. Isn't it the fault of the adults who were around him at 13, who prematurely pushed him into being a superstar, instead of letting him mature and become a great amateur player first? Any 13-year-old would be too immature to handle the situation in a healthy way.*)

Following are more stories, starting with Michael Avery, one of the first to be pulled into this trend. As a Southern California basketball phenom at an early age, Avery received a "tentative" college scholarship offer from Kentucky even before he enrolled in high school (2006). At the time, most sports analysts considered it to be a ridiculous offer, and even the University of Kentucky president and the NCAA president expressed their concerns. But the Kentucky coach who made the offer, Billy Gillespie, explained his thinking as, "If you're in recruiting, it's very, very competitive. You start earlier and earlier all the time because you're seeing guys earlier."

Once news of the unusually young scholarship opportunity spread, Avery was harassed by opponents, and reportedly felt tremendous pressure trying to live up to his image. He ended up switching high schools more than once, and he spent his junior year in high school not playing basketball at all, because of transer rules. His scholarship offer disappeared when Coach Billy Gillespie left Kentucky, and he had no contact with the new coach. Avery finished his senior year of high school with very few college basketball options, and ended up going to Sonoma State, a Division II school in California.

The same year that Kentucky's Gillespie made the offer to Avery, he offered a similar scholarship to a superstar ninth-grader named Vinny Zollo. Zollo didn't end up at Kentucky, either. He instead went to Western Kentucky and transferred after his freshman year to Furman University, where he was required to sit out a year due to the transfer.

At 12 years of age and 5'4"/ 120 lbs., Damon Harge was identified as the nation's top sixth grade basketball player in 2011—after getting exposure on *YouTube*. According to *RivalsHigh.com*, NBA player John Wall became a sort of mentor to Harge, but expressed concern: "All this is too serious for a 12 year old kid," said Wall. "He should be concentrating on having fun, but at the same time I understand why it's happening. What's he gonna say? 'No thanks, I don't want to be ranked right now?' It's not wrong and its not his fault. It's just the day and age we live in." (Harge continues to get attention, but won't be available until 2018.)

Seventh grader Katlyn Gilbert, described as "wildly talented" by *Yahoo!Sports* writer Cameron Smith, has already committed to a college basketball program, but, as Smith writes, "... Gilbert's early commitment feels so ludicrous ... Heck, there's a reasonable chance she might burn out on basketball long before she even reaches college."

Alabama made a scholarship offer to an eighth grade linebacker/running back named Dylan Moses. (LSU has also made an offer.) Though 6'1" and 215 pounds in eighth grade, it is still difficult to predict his development going forward—

physically, mentally or athletically. Nevertheless, according to *AL.com*, Dylan's father described the wooing process as Dylan being treated "like a five-star recruit." In addition, the Alabama staff supposedly believes that Dylan "has a chance to be the best player in the country ... in the Class of 2017."

Yahoo!Sports writer Frank Schwab offered this perspective on the Moses story: "While this story will get a lot of attention for its unusual nature, it doesn't mean that much. Moses doesn't have to sign anywhere for almost four years. Alabama and LSU aren't bound to their verbal scholarship offers. A lot can and will change. Moses really could turn out to be the best player in the 2017 class, and take one of these first two offers. Perhaps he'll find another school he likes along the way. Or maybe he'll find something else he'd like to do in college other than play football. A lot can change over four years in high school."

Schwab goes on to express hope that Moses "can be left alone for a while to lead a relatively normal life." But he doesn't have much hope that will happen.

Another example of young recruiting is happening in U.S. Soccer, where kids as young as 13 years old can be part of a year-round "youth development" program. American kids are also being invited to participate in soccer clubs in Europe, South America and Mexico, and they are going away from home to attend those programs at ages as young as 12 or 13.

BURNOUT

An article from EducatedSportsParent.com describes the three main theories about the causes of burnout in athletes. They are:

(1) The constant pressure to win, train, and perform leads to mental and physical exhaustion and stress.

(2) Feelings of entrapment because, so much money and time and energy have been invested in a particular sport, but the reward or enjoyment isn't there ... and it is felt that the cost of success outweighs the benefits.

(3) Feelings of disempowerment, resulting in a desire for personal control over one's life.

According to sports psychologists, burnout encompasses physical and/or emotional exhaustion, sport devaluation, frustration, and reduced athletic accomplishment. Eventually, burnout makes players want to either stop playing altogether, or they lose the motivation to work hard enough to play well.

Much has been written about burnout in kids who play sports, and most of the discussion relates to kids who focus on one sport too early—as opposed to kids who play sports, in general. Kids under the age of 18 who experience burnout reportedly either get bored with a particular sport, or become sick and tired of "it all" because they have been doing "it all" for a very, very long time.

Within any age group there is the question: *When giving up on a sport, are these athletes "burning out" or are they "peaking too early," or both?* Most of the time, even the athlete has a hard time understanding it. Some say it is a matter of losing motivation after achieving ultimate goals; some say it is simply taking the ability to participate in the sport for granted; some say that the stress of performing eventually breaks some athletes down; some say that priorities change with maturity; some blame the dramatic changes in coaching and playing style from one level to the next; some just get homesick, others get injured, etc.

Experts in both child development and youth sports are particularly concerned about burnout because it is happening to young athletes more frequently—and at younger ages. Fred Engh, the founder of the National Alliance for Youth Sports, and author of *Why Johnny Hates Sports,* explains that "we have reached the point of saturation—a vicious revolving door of never-ending seasons. Children can't even take a couple of months' hiatus from a sport for fear of falling behind their peers and being excluded from teams the following seasons."

In an insightful project called the "TOYA Study," researchers reported on the outcome of 203 elite athletes' lives 10 years after they were initially brought into the study. (They were 8 to 16 years old at the beginning of the study.) Out of the 203 elite athletes, 94 no longer played their sport, and only 14 were competing at a National or International level. The study concluded that *being an elite athlete was not a predictor of whether they will be a high level competitor when they are older.* Not surprisingly, these researchers also noted a "burnout syndrome" among many of the participants when they got older: many of the athletes reported that they realized that "there was more to life than practicing their sport" and/or "they wanted a social life."

There are many sports burnout cases in the typical high school, but most burned-out teenage athletes don't get much attention when they reject their sport—aside from their disappointed parents, coaches and friends. In contrast to teenagers, finding examples of college and professional sports burnouts is easy. Following are just a few examples:

As told in the book *Inner Excellence* by Jim Murphy, Alison Wagner started a very serious swimming career at the age of 7, which led to World Championship medals at the age of 16, and a silver medal at the 1996 Olympics—at the age of 19. Shortly after that competition, however, she developed an eating disorder and quit swimming completely—before her senior year in college. She explained, "I haven't been happy in the pool since I was 8 years old."

Former basketball star Chris Herren's burnout issues were so dramatic that they compelled Jonathan Hock to develop a documentary about him called *Unguarded*. Herren was an award-winning guard in high school and college, but he developed a serious drug problem and experienced more than one drug-related arrest. As filmmaker Hock explains, "Chris was always told that his destiny was to be a basketball player. He was never allowed to be who he was because he was always on track to be a star."

While not generally known as a "burned out" athlete, Andre Agassi, one of the best tennis stars ever, surprised most when he wrote in his autobiography called *Open: An Autobiography* that he "hated tennis from early childhood" and he felt "lonely on the court." He explains that he was pushed by his father to focus on tennis, and was eventually sent to a tennis camp at the age of 13—having to drop out of high school to go.

Describing himself in his young tennis years as "unhappy, stressed, and insecure about everything" as a result of the childhood pressure, he says that his life "was imposed on him, and tennis took away his childhood." Although Agassi was often quoted as "loving the game," he later claimed that was a lie he felt forced to tell.

Personally, I recall talking to a dejected mother once about the fact that her daughter had a Division I scholarship offer to play softball in college, but the daughter quit softball at the end of her junior year in high school, proclaiming she was "just done."

Marcus Dupree played football at Oklahoma after being highly recruited by Division I colleges, and he was soon named *Football News* Freshman of the Year. But by the end of his college freshman season, praise quickly turned to criticism, with complaints that he was out of shape and not working hard enough. He floundered, switched schools, quit football, went back to football ... but never succeeded any further. Were expectations too high? Did he burn out? Did the pressure crush him? Those questions are answered in the book that was written about him, *The Courting of Marcus Dupree*, and the *ESPN* documentary profile done about him in their "30 for 30" series entitled, "The Best That Never Was."

Then there are the "burnout turnaround" stories...........

Even the great Michael Jordan acknowledged burnout when he left the game of basketball at what was considered his peak. Explaining that he had "just lost his desire" to play basketball, he tried baseball, a sport he had always loved. But he didn't experience the same level of accomplishment as he did with basketball. Jordan eventually went back to basketball with a refreshed desire to play, and he led his team, the Bulls, to three more championships.

Ron Shelton, a filmmaker who produced a documentary about Michael Jordan called *Jordan Rides the Bus,* has said that Jordan "returned to basketball in 1995 a changed man. I think [he] learned. As an NBA superstar he'd taken it for granted; then he saw how hard it was to be a professional baseball player, these guys struggling in the minor leagues. And these were very, very good athletes. He learned to appreciate what he had."

Another of the burnout turnaround stories is that of Michelle Wie, who was entering amateur adult golf tournaments at the age of 10, and was the youngest player to make an LPGA cut—at the age of 14. She also played in a PGA tournament (against men) at the age of 14, and turned pro at 16. But being identified at a very young age as being a huge star in the female golf world, created extreme expectations to be put upon her by those close to her, and also by the media.

Wie stopped competing professionally at that young age, and says she had to consider what she really wanted to do. So she ended up going to Stanford for an academic education. As Wie once told Diane Pucin of the *Los Angeles Times,* "I'm making my own decisions, and going to Stanford was something I needed to do for myself. It was not a decision made for a golf career. It's been one of the first things in my life I did for myself. Growing up in the spotlight, playing tournaments when I was 12, I grew up a lot faster than maybe I had to. Going to college helped me be a normal 18 year old and that was something I needed. I needed something more to help me be well-rounded." She went on to say that, "I have more passion for the game now than I did when I was younger." (Wie is now back on the LPGA tournament circuit.)

Elena Delle Donne was the Basketball National Prep Player of the Year in 2008, her senior year of high school; and she was on her way to play for the top women's collegiate program at the University of Connecticut. However, as explained in a *USA Today* profile of Elena; because she had started playing basketball at the age of 4, and she had a personal trainer by the age of 9, Delle Donne felt "burned out" even before her senior year in high school. She also admitted that playing basketball her senior year wasn't enjoyable. In fact, basketball had started feeling like a burden to her before that year, so she wasn't even looking forward to playing college basketball. As a result—after only 2 days of summer school at Connecticut—she abruptly decided not only to leave the university, but to leave basketball completely.

Having played volleyball well enough in high school, Delle Donne chose to play college volleyball instead, and immediately transferred to the University of Delaware. After this critical one-year break, Elena eventually went back to basketball, and started playing again for the Delaware team. Said Delle Donne after going back to basketball; "I feel like I'm a 10 year old player again, just out there playing the game I love and being around my teammates." She is now playing in the WNBA.

Former tennis phenom Jennifer Capriati has often been described by sportswriters as "the poster child for athlete burnout," and though her story might be a bit extreme, it is reportedly not all that unusual. In a nutshell: Capriati's father was a tennis coach, and he started her playing tennis as a toddler. The Capriati family eventually moved to Florida to enroll in an intense training program, and Jennifer was good enough to turn pro at the age of 14 years old. Though she was a great tennis player, and became the youngest player to win the French Open junior title, she quickly cracked under the pressure she had been under her entire young life. She started to have minor run-ins with the law related to alcohol, parties, drugs, and shoplifting.

Jennifer finally took "a long break," explaining to the tennis community that she had "lost the enjoyment of the game." She was determined to stick with tennis, however, and was eventually named the ESPY Comeback Player of the Year. (She ended up retiring due to injuries.)

Finally ... it is up to parents and coaches to be sensitive to signs of burnout in a young athlete who might be focusing too much on only one sport. Symptoms are both physical and mental, and they might be subtle. Psychologists tell adults to look for unusual tension, fatigue, irritability, depression, expressions of anger, decreased energy level, problems sleeping, increased illness, inconsistent performance, and/or exhaustion.

QUITTING A SPORT/QUITTING ALL SPORTS

"If a horse is running away with you, the best thing to do is loosen the reins and the horse will slow down on its own. The harder you pull back on the reins, the faster the horse will go." (Barbara Hopewell, the mother of Olympic gold medalist swimmer Summer Sanders.)

The questions parents have regarding kids quitting a sport—or quitting sports altogether—are many, but the most frequent question that comes up is; *Should kids be allowed to quit a sport after they have started the season, or should they be forced to continue through the season?* The other question that frequently comes up is; *How should parents respond to a child who wants to give up sports completely?*

Many parents have insecurities about how to handle a "quitting situation," and it is difficult to know what is best for the child. Some parents feel they should follow the rule of "sticking with, and finishing, anything that is started—regardless." These parents make a child at least finish the full season of a sport out of respect for the team, the coach, and themselves. No parent wants to think of their child as a "quitter." But there are also parents who feel that it is pointless to participate in an activity if a child dislikes it, and they allow their children to quit.

Top experts at The Positive Coaching Alliance acknowledge that the "quitting decision" is a tough one, and they advise parents to first try to understand the reasons the child wants to quit the sport. They say, *Make the reasons to quit carry the most weight in the decision.* Professor and pediatrician Michael Bergeron also says, "There is no good answer on where to draw the line with the quitting decision. You need to know your child. If kids truly hate a sport, then let them quit. But maybe they just need some encouragement. Some 19- or 20-year olds may wish their parents had pushed them more to stick with sports when they were younger rather than giving them up."

Some kids will, right from the start, just enjoy any sport they are playing. There are those kids. Lots of them. But don't be too concerned if your child is not one of them. There are many children who reject a particular sport, or even more than one sport, for a variety of reasons—and parents will start to see a pattern in the reasons, such as: The child ....

> ... is not having fun;
> ... doesn't like to sweat;
> ... doesn't like standing and listening;
> ... is afraid of the ball;
> ... is afraid of teammates;
> ... is afraid of the coach;
> ... is bored;
> ... just likes playing in games, not practices;
> ... would rather be home playing video games;
> ... doesn't like the uniform;
> ... a piece of equipment is uncomfortable;
> ... and so on, and so on........

The list can go on and on, and you might be relieved to read this list if you recognize any (or many) of the complaints. Your child is not that unusual. In fact, according to many reports, 25-30% of kids drop out of sports altogether within the first 3 years of participating, and approximately 70% of kids quit youth sports completely by the age of 13 years old.

Researchers say that "not having fun" is the number one reason kids quit sports, so there is concern about kids quitting sports, particularly when it is for that reason. (Recall that "having fun" was previously described as the number one reason that kids want to play sports.) In particular, experts are fear that it is the pressure on kids to reach the top of their sport at far too young of an age that results in this complete "loss of fun"; They also stress that there are countless young athletes who would have continued playing sports and done well, if not for this pressure.

The bottom line is that there are no standard answers to the quitting questions. As with many other parent/child decisions, each one has to be made on an individual basis. Says Barbara Hopewell, the mother of an Olympian: "If you notice they are losing interest or enthusiasm is decreasing, make sure they are doing something they love, not doing it for a coach or a parent. Try a different sport or take a break. Once they realize it is their decision to continue, their interest may renew."

There are many examples of successful athletes who quit a sport at some point in their youth because they just didn't like it, or because they burned out on it at a young age. The following will give you real-world insight into the topic by showing you how certain successful athletes, and their parents, have handled some quitting decisions:

Jon Steller, once one of the best college volleyball players on a top-ranked team, told *NCAA.com* that he ran track in 6th grade, but got very nervous every time the gun went off, so it made him nervous to have to stand up on the starting line. He eventually quit running track and his mother signed him up for a volleyball camp. At first he wanted to also quit volleyball camp because he realized that it was all girls attending, but his mother made him stick with it—and he ended up loving the camp and the sport ... and obviously succeeding.

Young star golfer Beau Hossler was a very good Little League player, and had made the all-star team at 11 years old. But Beau decided to skip the All Star game so he could turn his focus to golf. His stepfather told the *Los Angeles Times* that, "His mother and I couldn't believe what he was doing. We sat him down, talked to him, told him he might not get another chance to play in a big game like this. But he wouldn't budge. We wouldn't call the All-Star coach. We made him do it. I think some of the neighbors thought there was some bad parenting going on."

Former Major League Baseball star Mark McGwire actually quit baseball his sophomore year in high school to play golf, and he was considered almost as good at golf as he was at baseball. (He obviously went back to baseball at some point.)

A unique "quitting story" is that of the great former NBA star Larry Bird. After an impressive high school basketball career, Bird went to Indiana University to play, but left the school and team after only a few weeks because he felt "lonely and isolated." (Bird grew up shy, in a small Indiana town.) He felt unwelcome by some of the Indiana players, and even by coach Bobby Knight—who was once quoted in a *SportsIllustrated.com article* as admitting; "Larry Bird is one of my greatest mistakes. I was negligent in realizing what Bird needed at that time in his life."

According to writer Seth Davis in his article, "When March Went Mad," Bird's uncles and his mother were furious that he left Indiana University and they wouldn't even speak to him for weeks. Nevertheless, after leaving the school, Larry stayed at home, worked as a trash hauler and played on an AAU basketball team. Eventually, Indiana State University staff got wind of what Bird was doing and started to recruit him. Though it was a difficult task to convince him to try college again, they did, and Bird's mother expressed her relief when she said, "... when [Indiana State's] Coach Hodges came the next year, it was like an answer to a prayer because I knew Larry had the talent but wasn't using it."

With this topic, I can provide a brief story which has the benefit of 20/20 hindsight. My son played tackle football for the first time when he was in 5th grade, and he was at the older end of the age range for his group. His experience was very positive, because he did not feel overwhelmed by the size or speed of his teammates and competitors. But the next year he was at the youngest age of the range of his football group, as he moved up into the next category. After the second or third practice he came to me and begged to quit football "right away" because he was *"terrified"* by the size of his teammates/tacklers. (I had never heard him use the word "terrified" before, so it got my attention.) Just as enlightening to me, he explained; "Last year it [football] was a game......this year it is survival!"

After some discussion, we made the decision that he could quit football "right away," even though we probably would not have let him quit another sport that easily. But when it came down to the possibility of physical and emotional injury, we had a different perspective.

My son is now 20, and he never went back to playing football, but he admitted a while ago that he wished he had stayed with it and played football longer—"because it would have been fun." Of course I immediately questioned our parenting when I heard that: Did we let him quit too soon? Did we shirk our duties to teach him a lesson in perseverance? So I asked him if he thought we made a mistake in letting him quit when he did, and he thought about it and replied, "No, because at the time I really, really wanted to quit, and I would have hated it. It's just now that I'm older that I wish I had played."

Even very successful athletes sometimes decide they have had enough, and they quit their sport long before they need to—leaving a lot more than confused parents and disappointed coaches in their wake. The NBA's Keyon Dooling is a prime example: After signing a new contract with the Boston Celtics, he decided to "retire" from the game of basketball, despite resistance from all of those around him. His explanation was described in a story by Jessica Camerato of *CSNNE.com*, which contained the following comments made by Dooling: "I was talking about it with my wife and with my pastors and all the people that are in my life, and nobody wanted me to retire," said Dooling. "It took literally a meltdown for everybody to see how serious I was about not playing ball anymore ... I just gave out too much and I wasn't getting enough back ..."

PARENTING AN ATHLETE

(IT AIN'T EASY TO DO IT RIGHT)

Dr. Shane Murphy teaches a college sports psychology course, and he routinely asks his students about their experiences in youth sports.

Says Murphy, "I'm always amazed. At least half the class will say, 'It was very negative because of my parents.' "

PARENTING AN ATHLETE

From the book *The Double-Goal Coach* by Jim Thompson, Director of The Positive Coaching Alliance:

"Here's the bottom line for parents. Your child's experience with youth sports will come to an end, and it may happen suddenly. If you are at all like me, you will look back and think, 'I wish I had enjoyed it more. I wish I hadn't obsessed so much about how well my child was performing, or the team's record, or whether he or she was playing as much as I wanted, or why the coach didn't play him or her in the right position.'"

Parents might think that the most important role they have in the life of their young athlete/child is the endless chauffeurring to practices and games. But there are far more important roles, such as simply being a supportive parent—which is harder than it sounds. In fact, some- times it seems like it takes a psychology degree to be a properly "supportive" sports parent.

Another important role is to be a well-behaved parent. Youth sports experts, pundits, psychologists, many parents, and anyone else coming into contact with sports parents are most alarmed at the escalating level of inappropriate behavior and meddling of certain over-anxious parents. As a result, there has been much written about problem parents and their negative, damaging influence on their children, and also on the image of youth sports, in general. Unfortunately, the stereotype of the crazy, over-involved sports parent is not far off the mark. But though it may seem like youth sports is full of these types of parents, it is a small minority.

Sports psychotherapist Susan Farber once wrote a piece online discussing the differences in various parents' approaches to their kids' sports efforts. As she explained, "Parents who have been athletes themselves seem to understand competition better. The parents who always wanted to be star athletes (but never were) have a more difficult time and can sometimes try to get their unrealized dreams met through their child." Experts also blame parents' unhealthy sports parenting on the chase of their dream that their child will be a professional athlete with wealth and status. Other parents are thought to be simply filling an emotional void in their own lives.

Along those lines, there have been many very good books written about the role of parents in youth sports, and there are several organizations and websites that offer advice and information. Since so much information is available and is provided by experts in parenting, coaching, child development, etc., this book will not reproduce much of what is already widely available and easily accessible.   (See Appendix)

What I would like to give you is real-world perspective on parenting an athlete, based on the comments and experiences of real-world parents of real-world successful athletes—along with the insights of the athletes, themselves. In addition, I will throw in just a few of those expert opinions.

THE SUPPORTIVE PARENT

Legendary basketball coach Mike Krzyzewski has said, "When someone believes in you it raises your confidence level and allows you to try things that are impossible to do by yourself." He also said, "Imagination gives you a destination. The greatest gift a coach can give a player, a teacher can give a student, and a parent can give their child is the opportunity to imagine great things. These dreams in childhood pave the way for future successes."

I have said it so many times to so many people, and I'll say it again: One of the most difficult tasks of a sports parent is how to be a "properly supportive" parent ... how to avoid saying the wrong things; how to say the right thing at the right time; how much (or how little) interest to show in practice, accomplishments, games, coaching, etc. Apparently the goal is for the child to know you care about what is going on—but does not feel like you care too much. It's a fine line to walk. It's difficult. But it's important.

In a survey conducted by the research team of Bruce Brown and Rob Miller, college athletes were asked for their worst memory from playing youth and high school sports. The overwhelming response: *The ride home from games with my parents.* And when the survey asked what their parents said that made them feel great, the overwhelming response then was, *I love to watch you play.* As explained by Brown and Miller, in the moments after a game, win or lose, kids desire distance in order to make a transition from being an athlete to being a child; and they prefer that parents transition from spectator or coach to just being Mom and Dad. (From a *Yahoo!Sports.com* article by Steve Henson)

This insight is extremely valuable. (Unfortunately I gained this insight too late ... so I want you to get it now.) I did, indeed, often experience the uncomfortable car ride situations described above. I felt like I could never say the right thing. Therefore, I whole-heartedly endorse Brown and Miller's insights.

Another important perspective provided by Jack Perconte (former MLB player and youth sports expert) also stresses that parents should not support a child who makes excuses for poor performance, and they should not make excuses themselves. Perconte explains that "excuse-making becomes contagious and it keeps athletes from accepting responsibility for their play. Even if there are reasons for poor play, it is better for parents and coaches to keep it to themselves. It is better to accept that the opponent was better that day. Saying things like, 'Hey, it was just one of those days, hang in there' or 'don't worry about it, you will get them next time' are good post game statements."

On the other hand, sports psychologist Dr. Rick Wolff advises parents to "skip the postgame analysis altogether" and just praise the *performance*. He also suggests that a parent simply remark on a specific play so the child knows that you were paying attention, and then move on. Dr. Wolff emphasizes the importance of resisting the temptation to produce even the slightest criticism.

Another extremely wise insight that I wish I had understood when my boys were young is the advice by many psychologists to *Praise EFFORT over ABILITY*. According to experts in the field, "Kids who are praised for effort show greater persistence and resilience in failure." This insight is also supported by a study that was conducted by respected psychologist Dr. Carol Dweck, in which students were given a puzzle to solve. Half of those students were praised for their intelligence and the other half were praised for their effort. In the end, *roughly 66% of the students who were praised for their intelligence (ability) chose the easy task—because they did not want to risk losing their "smart" label. But 90% of those who were praised for their effort chose the difficult test—because they wanted to prove just how hard working they were.* Makes perfect sense, doesn't it?

On the same topic, psychologist Dr. Peggy Drexler has written articles on *Huffington Post.com* and in *Psychology Today* that basically tell parents to stop complimenting our kids. In particular, Dr. Drexler points out that *research with children and families has indeed told us that praise has the opposite intended effect. It does not make children work harder, or do better. In fact, kids who are told they're bright and talented are easily discouraged when something is too difficult. She also wrote that by focusing too much on how we can build our kids' self-esteem and confidence, we're overlooking teaching them what real achievement means, and depriving them of knowing what it's like to feel the satisfaction of setting a high goal, working hard, and achieving it. Self-esteem really, truly comes as the result of achievement—in the classroom, on the field, at home—rather than false accomplishments.*

Do you think this applies to giving trophies to every participant in a youth sport, as opposed to just the winners? Some older parents, in particular, take issue with that practice because they grew up in a world where awards/trophies were only given to winners. The rest of the athletes had to accept that they didn't get one—but they could try harder to win one the next time. And that was ok. I'm not a psychologist, however, so ... I'm just throwin' it out there as food for thought.

The Cassel parents have apparently figured out how to be properly supportive, as all three Cassel brothers (Justin, Matt and Jack) have become professional athletes—even though neither of their parents played sports beyond high school. But the brothers feel that their parents had a tremendous influence in their professional careers simply through the support given each of them with their sports activities. Said Jack, in a *Los Angeles Daily News* interview: "This is what everyone dreams about when they're kids. But for us it was more than just a dream. We always thought it was possible. Mom would always tell us, 'Whatever you put your mind to you can attain.' It was just something embedded in our minds growing up. It gave us that mindset that we always thought this [success] was possible."

And "supportive parent" Bob Boss, who has two sons playing professional sports, told *sneakershock.com* that his advice for parents is: "Let them play. Don't push. If they want to play, fine, go to the games ... Enjoy them expressing themselves and being on the field, but know that sports is one of many paths that your kids can take. Support them and be their fans. There will be good times and bad times, you just gotta be there for them. It'll happen if it's supposed to."

Archie Manning, former NFL pro and father to football stars Peyton and Eli Manning, has said, "Everybody always used to praise me about how I'd sit in the stands and be calm. I understand daddies that holler and scream at the referees sometimes. You get excited, you want your son to do good, and you act like a fool and say stupid stuff. Fortunately, sometime at an early age in my embryonic times as a Little League daddy, I saw how stupid that looked. I thought, 'This is bad.' I don't ever want to look like this.' So I just shut up."

The mother of star pitcher CC Sabathia told *NorthCentralPA.com*: "My focus for CC when he was young was to enjoy childhood, have fun with his friends, and enjoy playing baseball. We didn't talk about professional baseball until late in his high school career." And Sabathia has said that his mom had a very big role in his success—she put catching gear on to catch his pitches in the back yard, and she also taught him toughness. He has also said that he remembers how important it was that his mom was in the stands in his youth baseball days.

Superstar NBA player Kobe Bryant grew up with a father who also played professional basketball, but he has said that his best memory about his father occurred when he was a teenager playing in a summer pro league in Philadelplhia. Explained Kobe in an interview, "I didn't score a point, and I was so disappointed. Dad came over and told me, 'It doesn't matter if you score zero or 100 points. We're going to love you.' Hearing him say that gave me so much confidence. I knew no matter what, he had my back."

The profoundly inspiring former MLB baseball pitcher, Jim Abbott, who succeeded in the sport with only the use of one hand, has often credited his parents for much of his success— explaining that they made him feel special, but treated him like every other kid.

In an article on the *We Play Moms.com* website, Barbara Hopewell, mother of Olympic swimmer Summer Sanders, wrote about her sports parenting approach while Summer was growing up. Describing how she made sure Summer understood that if she [Hopewell] was making an effort to support her, Summer's job was to be ready to go, she explained, "I made her responsible for getting herself up in the early morning (4:15 a.m.)," said Hopewell. She also stressed that she never bribed or rewarded Summer for reaching goals— teaching her that "self satisfaction and the feeling of accomplishment was her reward for a job well-done."

MOMS vs. DADS

Author Brooke de Lench writes in her book, *Home Team Advantage: The Critical Role of Mothers in Youth Sports*, that when it comes to youth sports, "Moms tend to concentrate on *youth*, dads on *sports*." Pointing out that the difference lies in how men and women are hard-wired, the crux of her book is that "women bring true balance to youth sports by focusing on the athlete more than on the win."

If you, as sports moms and dads, have not had any arguments at all with each other over your children's youth sports experiences and/or involvement, you are either very, very unusual or your child is very, very young. There are just inherent differences in perspective between fathers and mothers regarding many aspects of youth sports, and it is not unusual for mom/dad disagreements to occur over the right and wrong way to handle a sports-related situation.

One of the most common differences in perspective that moms and dads sometimes have with their children playing sports is the "fear of injury" that moms have, versus "less fear of injury" that dads have. Sometimes moms even get in the way of a child playing a sport like football because of the fear of injury.

Former Major League Baseball star Rickey Henderson's mom got in his way. As he told the audience in his Hall of Fame speech, "My dream was to play for the Oakland Raiders, but my mom thought I would get hurt playing football, so she chose baseball for me. I guess Moms do know best. Thanks Mom."

In a *USA Today* article, Ndamukong Suh, a 300 lb. NFL defensive tackle, explained that his mom was reluctant to let him play football; "I'm her youngest, and she didn't want her baby to get hurt. I had to explain to her that, if anything, I was going to be hurting somebody." (He still wasn't allowed to play until his sophomore year in high school.)

Writer Jacey Eckhart wrote a column that looked at the differences in the way fathers approach youth sports versus the way mothers look at sports. She described her own personal situation by pointing out the differences between her husband and herself. Explained Eckhart; "He [husband] sees youth sports as something our kids do as part of growing up. They will succeed and fail by the rules of the sport and their own gifts and the effort they put into it. When I look at youth sports, I see our children faced with frustration and joy and disappointment and self-reproach over what ought to be just a game."

Shaquille O'Neal's mom described her pre-game connection with her basketball son on *YahooShine*: "I would give him bubble gum before every game to calm his nerves. I would give him a kiss and tell him to have fun. That was our very special ritual." (So thaaaat's the secret!)

Country singing star Kenny Chesney told *Parade Magazine* about the impact sports had on his relationship with his father. "When my father and I didn't have anything in common and didn't talk about anything, there was always University of Tennessee football. There are a lot of fathers and sons out there like that. It was because of football that our relationship got better."

NBA player Kevin Love grew up with a dad in the NBA, and he credits his dad with the majority of his success. However, he admits that he and his dad did have a rivalry, saying, "When playing one-on-one, I never beat [my dad] until the 8th grade. And once I beat him, he stopped playing me."

Writer Steve Rushin once wrote a touching article in *Sports Illustrated* that talked about the importance of mothers to their successful athlete children. A few of his examples:

Former Twins slugger Kent Hrbek once explained the end of a slump by saying, "My mom told me to get my stinking elbows up higher, and Mom's always right."

When a reporter asked a 12-year old recovering cancer patient if he'd been given any words of wisdom before experiencing his "Make-A-Wish" dream of circling the bases at Safeco Field, he said, "My mom told me to run slow and wave." (Writer Rushin described this advice as "it may be the best motherly advice ever given, as true in life as it is on the base paths.")

Now, in contradiction to the stereotypical sports moms and sports dads ... One fun piece of information about the role of moms versus dads is that Kobe Bryant, one of the best basketball players of all time, credits his *mother* for his aggressive play and attitude—even though his father played professional basketball and has coached. Said Kobe, in a *Sports Illustrated* article, "My mom's the feisty one. She has that killer in her." He went on to say that from his father he got "the love for basketball, the ability to see the game on multiple levels, and a feeling for people."

And Greg Townsend, a highly recruited football player when he was in high school, told *SportsIllustrated.com* that, though his dad taught him all the football techniques (his father played football in the NFL), it was *his mom* that "taught me the passion and fire I have. She would always want me to go hard, be physical."

There is also the proverbial "soccer mom" (hard to define, but you know one when you see one). I did run across a humorous commentary about the species that was written by Peter Cary in *US News & World Report*. The article quoted Andrew Holzinger, athletic programs coordinator for Palm Beach County, who complained about the culture of "soccer moms." Said Holzinger: "Maybe all I wanted to do was have my daughter kick the soccer ball around; but Soccer Mom gets out on the field, and she has a new personality. She gets to bond with other parents about the lousy call ... Soccer Mom— she gets to have her own sport."

Finally ... during the 2012 and the 2014 Olympics, Procter & Gamble produced an entire series of very heart-tugging and sentimental commercials in which they portrayed the many different ways moms contribute to the success of their Olympic athlete children. During my research I read many of the comments written by readers of the P & G website that was built around this "Team Mom" theme, and the response to the commercials was very positive—among women. But it was interesting that there was a fairly significant male backlash toward these television spots, expressed in comments such as, *What about the dads--- where were they?; Didn't the dads go to practices and games, too?; Didn't the dads support and encourage and teach?; Didn't the dads work hard outside the home so the mom could take the kids to practices and games?; "Didn't a lot of dads stay home with the kids, too?*

BOTTOM LINE: Successfully parenting a young (and older) athlete requires the valuable, and different, perspectives of both moms and dads, it requires an expertise in psychology, and it requires time ... and loving effort ... and support.

THE OVER-INVOLVED PARENT/PRESSURE FROM PARENTS

Drew Henson was a quarterback at Michigan the same time Tom Brady was there, and, by most accounts, he was more skilled than Brady. But Henson's dad was said to be quite "over-involved" in Drew's career, and controlled "everything"—to the point that he was asked to stay away from practices. Henson's sports career ended up being jagged, as he moved between baseball and football—and he is now retired.

According to an interview in *Sports Illustrated,* Henson made "misguided athletic career choices" along the way, and he, himself, acknowledged that his choices were not always his. Said Henson; "If I'm fortunate enough to be a parent someday, I won't try to control every situation that my child may be put into as an athlete—not try to dictate every time line or micromanage every aspect of the child's development."

Following is a real-world letter written to the advice column "Ask Amy": *Dear Amy, I am a 12-year-old girl with three older brothers (13, 19 and 20). My dad pushes us to play sports, even if we don't like it. Right now I am playing soccer, which I enjoy. He signed me up for softball without notifying me. I don't like this sport, but my dad is pushing me. I want to quit, but it is hard for me to talk to my dad because he ignores what I say. When I have soccer practice, I get so excited, but when I have softball, it ruins my day. I do not want to continue playing, but I don't know how to tell my dad."*

The unhealthy over-involvement and pressure that parents impose upon young athletes is insidious, basically because most parents are not aware that they are even putting the pressure on. It comes in many forms, and is often found in the simple, well-intentioned comments made in efforts of support and encouragment. *But what is over-involvement? What is pressure, specifically? What is the difference between pressure vs. expectations vs. goals vs. expecting a complete effort, etc.? And, given that the level of "pressure" that affects one child may not have the same impact on another child ... what is a parent to think or do?*

The best way to explain and discuss this concept is through real-world examples of over-involvement and pressure situations, and the impact they have had. Maybe you'll recognize a familiar side-effect or style ... or maybe you'll recognize yourself.

As tennis coach and former professional tennis player Hank Pfister has written, "When I was a kid, parents would drop us off at the courts for the day and rarely ever watched us practice. And they only attended our more important tournament matches. Kids were free to enjoy the game with their friends, to develop a sense of personal competence in their skills, to experiment on their own with a variety of shots, and to develop their own internal motivation to excel. Today, there are parents that watch every practice, often coaching and prodding through the fence. Parents often sit on the side of the court at private lessons, or even worse, make comments to the child during the lesson. Parents and coaches are causing the deterioration of today's athlete's ability to think on their own, be versatile, well- rounded, self-motivated, confident and team oriented."

In the same article, Pfister asks over-involved sports parents to really ask themselves, "Who are you doing this for?" He goes on to ask parents, "Even if you are just doing it for a college scholarship, is it worth ruining a child's adolescence and possibly your long-term relationship with that child for the sake of your goals? If everything you do with this child revolves around the sport being played ... you are missing the point of sports."

According to a Seth Davis column in *Sports Illustrated,* the mother of high school and college basketball standout Larry Drew II was such a "meddler" in all aspects of his sports career that she "would call the coaches to complain about how many minutes her son was playing or how many shots he was getting." And, worse yet, her "meddlesome tactics resulted in Drew's younger brother getting booted off his high school squad."

The following "anonymous" commentary was taken from the comments section of a blog about youth sports, and it is certainly worth passing on. "I have just retired from high school wrestling coaching after 15 years to return to the youth level. The club that I built starting 23 years ago created the best high school results in the history of the program. Some over-zealous parents took over the club, pushed tournament competition on 5, 6 and 7-year-olds and they have virtually destroyed our entire program. The kids quit by 5th grade, and ... the youth club put zero kids into our Junior High program this year. This is a tragedy that is happening all over the country."

And "straight from the horse's mouth": In one study where young athletes were asked to comment on the role of parents in their sports play, one child made the following comment: "Whenever you get yelled at, you really can't do better. It gets on your nerves when people yell at you. You shouldn't pressure a kid, because they get all tensed up and don't play to their potential."

As NBA star Joakim Noah has said, "I always see that when I go back to New York and go to the park and play basketball or something and see a father pushing his kid and you can tell the kid is not having fun. He's going to stop playing when he's 14 or 15."

In his book, *Will You still Love Me if I Don't Win?*, author and sports counselor Christopher Anderson writes, "Parents who don't have an emotional awareness do not fully relate to the pressures and fears their children are experiencing. They often put pressure on them to straighten up and do a better job, which only increases their children's concerns and often causes them to hold back even more."

This letter was written by a mother to *Los Angeles Times* sportswriter Eric Sondheimer. (With dismay, Sondheimer insists it's a real letter!): *My son, who is 4 1/2 years old (4 feet, 60 pounds) plays golf, tennis, soccer, T-ball, basketball, swims and is in a running club. The private elementary school kindergarten acceptance letters came and we would love to know which of the following have the best elementary sports programs. We have to make a decision by April 12.*

David Leadbetter, famed golf instructor and founder of the Leadbetter Golf Academy, is quoted by Kevin Cook in his book, *Driven*, as saying, "Some parents act so pushy that the overbearing, high-pressure parent is becoming as much a golf cliche' as it used to be in tennis." And in the same book, sports psychologist Jim Loehr says, "Half of my work is with parents, and most of them don't have a clue. They push and push until the kid hates golf."

In his book *The Ripken Way*, baseball's legendary Cal Ripken, Jr. explains, "All sports parents need to have a strong sense of patience. Indeed, praise and patience go hand in hand when working with kids. If you don't give them the patience they need, then kids will run the risk of just getting frustrated. When they become frustrated, there's a good chance they will walk away from that sport."

A *Los Angeles Times* column about Olympic shot putter Jessica Cosby that described her passion for her sport, ended with the columnist, Sandy Banks, writing, "I'll be thinking of the lesson she (Cosby) and her mother offer parents like me; You don't have to nag a future Olympian. If you have to threaten your kids to make them practice, or drag them off the couch to make it to a lesson or a game, perhaps 'we' are pursuing the wrong dream."

The 2005-2006 NHL Rookie of the Year, Patrick O'Sullivan, had serious issues with his father, who had, himself, been a minor league hockey player. The father was reportedly emotionally and physically abusive to Patrick when it came to hockey, starting at the age of 9, and it got worse as Patrick got older and more involved in hockey. The problems in the relationship escalated to the point that O'Sullivan eventually filed charges against his father and his situation became a well-known drama in hockey circles. As a result, professional teams were actually reluctant to even consider O'Sullivan because they didn't want to have to deal with that level of drama. So, by all accounts, it affected Patrick's draft position: he was eventually drafted in the second round, but most agree he would have gone in the first round, otherwise.

In a *USA Today* online survey, 80% of adults said that youth sports today can be too competitive. And when the survey asked who the culprit is, a surprising *78% (of the 80%) said it is the parents, 14% said it's the coaches and only 6% claimed it is the kids who are too competitive.* (Of course those parents in the 78% weren't talking about *themselves*—they were referring to *other parents.*)

Note to parents: It is a fairly "open secret" in youth sports that youth coaches base a great deal of their player selection on who the parents of the kids are, how cooperative and pleasant the parents are, and the level of pressure the parents put on the kids and coaches. Also, the attitude the coach has towards a child can be heavily influenced by the attitude of the parents. Trust me. I've heard it acknowledged by many, many coaches in various youth sports. (Youth coaches are only human, after all.)

Finally ... there is no better way to end this chapter than to reproduce the humorous sign that the park district of Buffalo Grove, Illinois, posted (permanently) at their public parks as a "real-world" message to anyone at the parks. It follows:

Things for coaches, parents and spectators to keep in mind while children are playing sports on our fields.....

* This is a game being played by children.

* If they win or lose every game of the season, it will not impact what college they attend or their future income potential.

* Of the hundreds of thousands of children who have ever played youth sports in Buffalo Grove, very few have gone on to play professionally. It is highly unlikely that any college recruiters or professional scouts are watching these games;

   So, let's keep it all about having fun and being pressure free.

PARENTS GIVING ADVICE TO KIDS

Anyone who has been a parent of kids older than 10 knows that there is a point in a child's life where they absolutely do not want their parents' advice—about anything. In fact, they might even go in the complete opposite direction of the advice in an effort to reject it. Right? This is particularly true when it comes to kids and sports, so youth sports experts strongly caution parents to leave feedback and advice to the coaches.

Rest assured that sports psychologists say it is very normal for young athletes to have difficulty receiving feedback and criticism from parents. Even parents who have had good experiences coaching their kids' teams when the kids were young eventually reach a point where they just shouldn't be coaching their own kids anymore. It might also be comforting to know that even professional athletes run into this very problem with their own children.

A *Golf World* article talked about the daughter of tennis star Ivan Lendl, who was a successful golfer; but she quit the game for about a month because, as she explained, "I was sick of my dad riding my back on everything. I was rebelling against him." But she came back to golf after a short time, demanding her independence and telling her dad, "I don't want you to tell me anything unless I ask. And, slowly, I kind of asked him." (Lendl's wife backed up the story, explaining; "There comes a point when the child takes the lead.")

Not surprisingly, the sons of former superstar quarterback Joe Montana play football, but it might be surprising to know that

Montana and his sons have to deal with the same issues as everyone else. As Joe Montana, himself, admitted to the *San Jose Mercury News*; "The minute I start watching them [his kids] practice, I want to talk to them. You don't want to get in their way but you think ... 'If I could just help them a little bit here and there.' " But as Montana's son explained, "It's weird to other people, but he's our dad and we had the same reaction everyone does when their dad tells them something. We don't want to listen. It took us a few years to realize he knows what he's talking about."

As NBA player Joakim Noah wrote on his website, *JoakimNoah.org*; his father, former professional tennis great Yannick Noah, is "always telling me, 'Calm down, take a deep breath, you're not breathing enough.' " So Joakim responds to him, "All you've got to do is just chill out, man, drink a couple of beers, watch the game and let me play." Added Joakim, "He stresses me out."

In a study of elite youth baseball players, one young athlete said, "The ideal parent just lets you play by yourself because you obviously know more than the parent. Let me do what I'm doing and you [the parents] just cheer. Let the coach coach me."

And finally ... a very wise psychologist, Dr. Steven Hunt, once told me, myself—quite succinctly and effectively— *Unsolicited advice is usually interpreted as criticism.*

PARENT BEHAVIOR

According to the National Alliance for Youth Sports, parent violence at kids' athletic events quadrupled just between 2000 and 2005! (And it keeps getting worse.)

The topic of parent behavior in youth sports (misbehavior, to be specific) has seen lots of headlines over the past several years, with the growing frequency and intensity of incidents. Sports programs are intent on finding ways to control and calm parent behavior, such as "sportsmanship training sessions" and "parent contracts and rules." Of course, as with most things human, it is only the very small minority that causes the very big problems. But what significant problems they are, nevertheless!

One disturbing trend is the reported increase of "disappointment lawsuits" against athletic coaches and officials—parents suing coaches, school districts, and other sports administrators for perceived injuries against their young athlete child. For example, one parent sued a high school baseball coach for making his son pitch too much—damaging his arm and "ruining his chance for a college scholarship." Another sued a high school coach for doing a poor job of showcasing his child athlete to scouts and colleges; while yet another parent sued a college coach after his football star son wasn't named starting quarterback, after the coach had promised him the position. And, in one of the more ridiculous cases (though, aren't they all ridiculous?) ... a parent sued for $1,500,000 when his son was moved down from varsity to junior varsity level. The move supposedly affected his future professional earnings!

Most of these suits don't go very far, but the mere fact that they are even filed says quite a bit about the level of parent involvement, poor attitude, and poor behavior present in the real world of today's youth sports programs.

The more common, smaller problems with parent behavior are caused by a "larger minority," and they are plentiful and varied. But don't feel like such a terrible parent if you happen to slip once by exhibiting sports parent behavior that you're not particularly proud of. It can happen to any parent—even a professional athlete like David Beckham. According to Beckham, himself, he was red-carded at his son's soccer game and told to get out of the park by the referee. The reason: The ref gave a 7-year-old player a penalty and sent him off the field, Beckham challenged the ref's actions, and the referee responded as he would to any other "meddling" soccer parent.

In a clinical research study reported in the *Journal of Sport Behavior,* it was determined that "background anger" on the sidelines of a youth sport activity is distressing to the children playing, and the younger the children, the more distressing the behavior. This study also pointed out that children are most disturbed by adult-to-adult anger during a youth sports activity. Most enlightening was the fact that children and officials reported angry attitudes from the sideline parents as occurring much more frequently than the sideline parents reported, themselves.

PARENT/COACH INTERACTION

One other area where parents can be very supportive of their young athletes is in showing respect and support for the coach. It is a great example to set and can even set the tone for the entire team. If a positive attitude and a cooperative, trusting relationship is developed between an "influential" parent on the team and the coach, there is bound to be less detrimental parent behavior overall.

There are a number of stories of parent/coach conflicts among even the very young sports teams, and there are untold numbers of coaches who have quit coaching because of the parents—in spite of their love for the kids and the sport. Parents need to remember that these coaches are volunteers, they are adults, and they are generally parents, as well. In most cases, the coaches are doing the best they can—sometimes with very little athletic experience themselves. But they did step up to the plate.

That's all I am going to say about coaching, as there are wonderful resources on the topic; some are listed in the Appendix. But ... PLEASE HAVE MERCY ON YOUR CHILD'S VOLUNTEER COACH! (And don't sue them.)

PARENTS COACHING THEIR OWN KIDS

Although this book stays away from discussing coaching in detail, it is worth briefly addressing the issue of coaching your own kids—as there are many questions about the impact of that. Any of you who have had this experience probably agree that coaching your own kids can be extremely rewarding and fun ... and perhaps difficult. And as the kids get older, it becomes harder. Thankfully, though, the rewards outweigh the difficulty for most, or else there would be no youth sports at all. (Warm personal thanks go out to ALL of you youth coaches!) There does come a time, however, when it's time to stop coaching your own kids, and most parents eventually see the writing on the wall. (See section on "giving advice to children.")

One of the toughest parts of coaching your own child's youth sports team is the opportunity for teammates and parents to cry favoritism; and it happens, no matter how irrational or unwarranted. It's an easy excuse for any child who doesn't get to be the star or for any loss the team may experience. It comes with the territory and it is best to address it very early on with your child and with the other athletes and parents on the team. (Take comfort in knowing that it happens with the kids of high school, college and pro coaches too.)

Cody Hawkins was starting quarterback under his father, coach Dan Hawkins, while at the University of Colorado, and he had to face the controversy of being the coach's son—even though he had been ranked #13 among quarterbacks nationally. But Cody told *USA Today* that he was ready for the controversy because,

"Growing up I've always kind of been in the spotlight, anyway. I'm playing Pop Warner football and people are blaming mistakes on me being the coach's kid." Nevertheless, in a telling comment, Hawkins responded to his father's firing as head coach by admitting to the *Denver Post* that he "always wondered what it would be like not to be identified as the coach's son."

Another conflict that arises in coaching your own kids is that they (and your spouse) sometimes perceive that you are being harder on your kids than on the other kids—and sometimes you probably are. It's hard not to be, when you're under such scrutiny. But whether you are or not doesn't matter; it is the *perception* that you are that matters, and it has to be addressed, not ignored or dismissed. Fear not though: St. Louis Cardinal Chris Carpenter, for one, has said that even though his dad, as coach of his Little League teams, was tougher on him than the other players, he was still his favorite coach.

VOLUNTEERING ... GETTING INVOLVED

According to the National Alliance for Youth Sports, 70% of youth sports organizations in North America are administered by volunteers, whose only qualification or requirement is "the willingness to do the job." So there would be no youth sports activities for your children without the willingness of parents to volunteer. Please consider doing it yourself, if you have the time. You will find that unexpected fun, satisfaction, and a sense of community comes along with it. Your children will notice and appreciate your efforts, as well. It's a great example to set for them.

Unfortunately, the majority of parents are reluctant to volunteer, and coaches/managers often have to do some heavy recruiting and deliver anguished pleas to get parents involved. For many parents it is fear of the unknown that holds them back. They are afraid they will have to do something they don't want to do; or something that takes too much time; or something they don't know how to do. But, in reality, there are few volunteer positions that are overwhelming, and few that require expertise.

Also, responsibilities on youth sports teams are broken up so that they can be spread around more easily. And ... here's a helpful hint: By volunteering "right away" you can choose what you want to do. The worst jobs are left for those who volunteer last or reluctantly get recruited late. (That is a "veteran's secret" I just shared.)

SO STEP UP. VOLUNTEER!

WHAT SEPARATES "THE BEST" FROM "THE REST" ???

"There is no such thing as a bad athlete. There are some athletes who mature faster, some athletes that develop faster, and some athletes that figure it out faster. But given the chance to properly develop, recruit and hold muscular positions in the manner a muscle was intended, any athlete can improve to a level way beyond his or her expectations or the expectations of others ...

There are some kids who 'just have it' and seem able to do it all. If your child doesn't 'have it,' don't worry. It's no indication that your child can't or won't succeed to high levels in sports. It just may take longer ... some kids mature faster than others ... some children advance quicker physiologically than others ... but as time continues, the playing field starts becoming more level."
(From *Raising an Elite Athlete* by Dr. Malcolm Conway)

IS IT TALENT?

CAN SUCCESS BE PREDICTED?

Would you trust a genetic test that would tell you if your child was born to be an elite athlete? Would you even test your child? What would you do if the test was negative? Would you tell your child the results? Would he/she still play sports? Would you treat your child differently when playing sports if they tested positive—or negative?

Well, believe it or not, scientists have actually come up with a genetic test that they claim can tell if a child is "born to be an elite athlete." Specifically, they have identified several genes that may play a role in determining strength, speed, and other aspects of athletic performance. For example, one gene that the test identifies is linked to "explosive force." But this gene exists in 80% of the general population. And, interestingly, a Spanish Olympic long jumper who relies on his "explosive force" actually tested negative for the gene.

It is safe to say that, in most cases, athletic success cannot be predicted—particularly at young ages. In fact, many high school coaches of eventual professional athletes have admitted that they didn't see significant potential in those athletes until about their junior year. And even at that age, it is said to be difficult to make a dependable prediction.

Making the above point specifically, NHL scout Tony Bonello told *Hockey Digest,* "I can assure you that scouting is not a science. And the reason is you are making decisions on 17- and 18-year-old players. These young men are not mature hockey players, and there is no assurance that they will be as good at maturity as they were at 17 and 18 years of age. And vice versa."

The high school coach of NBA star Jeremy Lin told *ESPN* that he never believed he was coaching a future NBA player when he coached Lin.

Tennis coach Robert Lansdorp, who helped develop superstars Tracy Austin, Pete Sampras, and Maria Sharapova, among others, pointed out in a *USA Today* article that it is difficult to predict success in tennis at a very young age and that he "couldn't tell Maria [Sharapova] was going to win Wimbledon when she was 14-15." He went on to say that "none of his students looked like potential champions before they were teenagers. And even then, some didn't."

Chase Utley, considered one of the best MLB players today, was cut from his high school baseball team his first season. His father was quoted in a *Los Angeles Times* article as saying that "he [Utley] was a good player, but nothing that would have suggested that he was going to be the guy that would go to the show. Chase wasn't a kid who was on the USA baseball teams, under 16 and 18 teams and stuff like that."

Even the father of superstar Matt Kemp has admitted; "He [Matt] has surpassed everything everybody thought he would have done by now." (from a *Jockbio.com* article)

I am also adding my 2-cents, based on my many years of exposure to young athletes. I can attest that there were several superstar athletic kids I observed when they were 7 – 12 years old who, as teenagers, were either not playing any sports at all, playing sports just recreationally, or they eventually became fat or lazy or drug addicts or devoted musicians or passionate writers, etc. By the same token, I have seen kids who eventually became sports superstars who none of us adult observers would have predicted to shine in athletics. All you have to do, yourself, is think back to your young days in school: where are those superstar young athletes now that you witnessed back then?

Unfortunately, there are countless young athletes who end up quitting a sport, or quitting sports altogether, because they feel they are — and will always be — too small, too big, too fat, too slow, too unfocused, too lazy, etc. to play sports. And because most parents and coaches probably have the same perception about the limitations of kids' size and/or mental development on their abilities, it is difficult for these kids to believe they can go on successfully. In order to get over that perception, a young athlete either has to have an inner drive that won't accept "no" or "quitting" or "failure," or he/she has to have a special coach or parent who strongly encourages effort, despite the *perceived* physical or mental limitations. (See chapter on successful athletes who were underestimated.)

Again ... there is no way to predict the potential for a child to become an elite athlete when they are still a child. In fact, that is one of the key reasons I wrote this book: to make that very point, and to provide that perspective to those who wonder about it, or those who might think differently. The bottom line is that there are several key variables involved in the eventual success of a young athlete.

NATURAL TALENT

Many people believe college and professional athletes, in any sport, were born with something special, something different, something pre-ordained—particularly when it comes to their body type and/or athletic abilities. Doesn't everyone use the terms "talent" or "natural talent" constantly when talking about a successful person, and particularly when talking about successful athletes? But what is talent?

The subject of "natural talent" is one of the most controversial topics in this book. Nevertheless, one of the reasons this book was written was to adjust both parents' and kids' incorrect perceptions about the idea of "natural talent." And this is such an important topic in youth sports because the perception of the talent reality or myth is critical to the way a child—and parents and coaches—approach the child's sports experience.

In an article in the *BBC News Magazine* called "The Myth of Talent vs. Effort," writer Matthew Syed stresses the importance of emphasizing to children that it is *effort* that yields results, *not talent*. He goes on to ask, *Why would a child be motivated to work hard if he already thinks he has the talent to achieve in sports?* and, *Why would a child be motivated to work hard if he thinks he doesn't have the coordination/talent for sports?*

An interesting angle to this whole discussion is the fact that successful athletes are said to slightly resent the premise that they have "natural talent," because the idea diminishes their own reality that they worked very, very hard for their success. For example, Geoff Colvin, author of the book *Talent is Overrated*, told Charlie Rose in an interview that legendary golfer Sam Snead notoriously resented that people perceived his swing to be a "natural swing" because his swing was, in fact, a result of his very hard work. In the same interview, Colvin also pointed out that "people want to believe that Tiger [Woods] has an extraordinary gift, but they have to remember that he had been working hard under professional teachers for 17 years [before he became extremely successful]."

This is not to say that there are no really unique athletes who do "have it all" and were born with superior physical attributes — great bodies, special muscle development, intense hand-eye coordination, a "mind for sports", etc. (As the old basketball adage goes, "You can't teach height.") There are, of course, successful athletes who do have a physical and/or mental advantage over others. But the point to be made is that it is probably only a moderate percentage who are truly "gifted." And think about this: there are just as many equally gifted athletes who don't succeed, or go very far.

The *real* point to be made is that an athlete does not have to have a "natural" ability or athletic "gifts" to succeed. By the same token, those with athletic gifts or talent may not necessarily succeed.

There are also athletes who might have a somewhat small advantage, such as height, strength, etc., and they end up getting an inordinate amount of attention just because of that advantage — which makes them better, more confident and more competent athletes in the long term. This is somewhat of a "Catch-22 effect"; or, as author Geoff Colvin calls it, a "multiplier effect."

Following are some who are widely described as "naturally gifted" athletes:

NBA star Vince Carter is said to have special vertical jumping capabilities that exceed most of his NBA peers, and he was already dunking basketballs when he was 6 feet tall.

NFL wide receiver Calvin Johnson was described by his Georgia Tech college coach as, "He's a once-in-a-lifetime player. I've never had one this big, this fast, with this good hand-eye coordination. That's the stuff you can't teach." But, on the other hand ... NFL Trainer Tom Shaw told *USA Today* that, after training Johnson his rookie year, he put Calvin Johnson in a special category—but not because of his physical abilities. Said Shaw about Johnson, "I've never seen a guy with this guy's work ethic. He's a different breed."

Baseball's Josh Hamilton is said to have been unusually "athletic and coordinated" at the age of 7. (He also has 20/10 vision with great hand/eye coordination.)

Swimmer Michael Phelps is said to have a body that is uniquely suited to swimming skills—in both size and proportion.

Olympic swimmer and gold medalist Missy Franklin has Size 13 feet that her dad refers to as her "built-in flippers."

Star baseball player Johnny Damon's high school coach, Danny Allie, told *Sports Illustrated Kids*, "No question he was probably the most athletically gifted player I had ever had. He was a man among boys. There was just a presence about him that made him different."

One take on "natural talent" was expressed by Hall of Fame wide receiver Jerry Rice in an *ESPN Radio* interview. In that interview, Rice candidly described his frustration at watching Randy Moss play football because he [Rice] believed that Moss had more "talent" or natural ability than he did—but that Moss wasn't using it to its full extent. Explained Rice, "I was not as talented [as Moss] and I had to work harder. To see a guy with that much talent not give it 100%, it was almost like a slap in the face. But Randy was Randy. He could have been one of the greatest if he had worked just a little bit harder. I don't think he wanted to give it 100%." (Moss did rank third in all-time receiving touchdowns at the time.)

Sometimes body type and/or size is wrongly credited as being "natural talent," when, in fact, one athlete might just have a body that is more suited to sports than another. Is that talent?

One sport might require specific physical attributes moreso than others. For example, according to journalist and former competitive swimmer Lynn Sherr, swimming is a sport where physical characteristics can, indeed, separate the best from the rest. In particular, Sherr claims that much of the difference between Olympic swimmers and others is their height, with most of them measuring over 6 feet tall. In addition, says Sherr, wingspan in a swimmer makes a distinct difference in ability— and interestingly, many highly accomplished swimmers tend to be double- jointed and/or pigeon-toed.

Nevertheless, body type alone will not create a successful athlete in any sport—even swimming. It helps, and there are many examples of that. Major League Baseball's Bubba Starling, for one, is an athlete who is said to have always had strength and height on his side: as a 6'5", 190 pound senior in high school, he was described as having wiry strength and tremendous athleticism. Starling was one of those who did dominate sports in childhood and who went on to a successful professional career.

There was a show on *Fox Sports Network* (later picked up by *ESPN*) called *Sport Science* that looked at the accomplishments and abilities of successful athletes from a scientific viewpoint. According to John Brenkus, the host and creator of the show, one goal of the show was to dispel the theory that professional athletes just *wake up and get out of bed as talented as they are.* Said Brenkus, in a *Westlake Magazine* interview; "Although there are naturally gifted athletes, blessed with the genetics of being bigger or stronger, at the elite level it's all about hard work." For example, he pointed out that "Drew Brees is one of the best quarterbacks, but one of the least impressive physically. His brain and work ethic are what separate him."

The relationship between hard work and talent has been written about extensively, and it is being researched more and more in scientific settings. There have been dramatic leaps in understanding the brain over the past several years, and expert views about the nature of *ability, talent, skill, learning, motivation*, etc. are changing along with the research.

In the bestselling book *Freakonomics*, the authors Steven D. Levitt and Stephen J. Dubner addressed the issue of, *Where does talent really come from?* To answer that question, they reviewed and described some fascinating research conducted by Anders Ericsson, a psychology professor at Florida State University who is involved with a group of scholars trying to answer the similar question: *When someone is very good at a given thing, what is it that actually makes him good?* In general, their research concludes that *expert performers are nearly always made, not born.* Or, put another way: *The trait we commonly call talent is highly overrated.*

In the previously referenced article on this topic by Matthew Syed, "The Myth of Talent vs. Effort," it was written that "dozens of studies have found that top performers learn no faster than those who reach lower levels of attainment. The difference is simply that high achievers practice for more hours. This is not to deny that some kids start out better than others—it is merely to suggest that the starting point in life is not particularly relevant." Syed goes on to explain that "over time, with the right kind of practice, we change so dramatically. It is not just the body that changes, but the anatomy of the brain."

In his book, *The Talent Code*, author Daniel Coyle writes about his findings and observations when he traveled the world to see why athletes from Europe and Asia were doing so well. As he told the *Los Angeles Times,* he discovered "one universal truth": "It's pretty simple," explains Coyle. "You practice more, you get better. Here in the U.S., we've fallen in love with the idea that athletic talent is a gift. That's a beautiful idea, that a baby is born with a gift, that a Michael Jordan had a divine spark, or that Serena Williams is so gifted that she can just go out and sell tennis shoes. But guess what? Turns out that idea is fundamentally wrong."

The previously mentioned book, *Talent is Overrated*, also takes on this issue of natural talent head-on, addressing the misconception that people have a "gift" of natural talent and that "you either have it or you don't." And the book's author, Geoff Colvin, basically makes the same argument about success, *in general*, as well as success *in sports*: that there are many variables to success, and what people might consider to be "natural talent" or "natural body type" or "natural whatever" are really not natural at all.

It is also very interesting to note that in his book, Colvin discusses the "pushback" on his arguments about talent that he experienced when his book was published. Many people had a bit of skepticism and were reluctant to accept some of the concepts he promoted. Lots of people wanted to "shoot the messenger." Colvin explains this reaction by pointing out that people just naturally resist accepting this talent argument, out of self-protection of the ego. In other words, "If inborn gifts aren't the cause of success, then each of us must be responsible for his or her own achievement."

Finally ... in the words of sports psychologist Dr. Bob Rotella: "The fact is, we don't know exactly how much talent anyone has. Talent is a mixture of physical and mental qualities that is immeasurable. The question is not whether you have great talent ... The question is whether you're willing to put in the time and energy to develop the talent you have."

The subject of talent/natural talent is a fascinating one and the topic has obviously filled books just by itself. Readers are encouraged to read books like Colvin's and Coyle's in order to understand the issue more deeply. Their insights can support the development of realistic expectations in youth sports.

CONSISTENCY

There are college athletes in any sport who—on any given day— would be able to hold their own against a professional in the same sport. The star college athletes, however, generally don't play as well *consistently*.

The following story about baseball great Derek Jeter falls along the same lines. Jeter told *Men's Health Magazine* that he struggled his first year in the minor leagues, making 56 errors. But he had already been promised an opportunity to go to a major league training camp his second season, and once he got there he had a revelation: "I was only there two weeks, but I got an opportunity to see these players," said Jeter. "And that's when I said to myself, 'It's not that they're throwing 100 miles an hour faster, or hitting 400 feet longer. They're just doing things more consistently.' And then I thought, 'Well, I can do some of those things. Not as consistently, but I'm capable of doing it.' That was the defining moment that helped turn my career around."

Successful athletes play well ... consistently.

Consistency also implies dependability, which NHL goalie Patrick Roy discussed in an interview in *Kukla's Korner*. Said Roy, "I think the position [goalie] demands that you stand tall and say, 'Hey guys, I'm there.' You don't want the players thinking, 'okay, is the goaltender going to be OK tonight? Is he going to be shaky?' You want to make sure that they guys go, 'Okay, we're ok. Patty is in the net. He's going to have a good game, and all I have to worry about is play hard as a team.' "

IS IT PHYSICAL?

Of course it's physical ... *but only to a point.*

EARLY PHYSICAL AND/OR MENTAL DEVELOPMENT ----*(EARLY BLOOMERS)*

As stated in an article on *MomsTeam.com*, *"Research suggests only 1 in 4 children who are star athletes in elementary school will still be stars when they reach high school. Predicting whether a pre-teen athlete will be a good enough high school athlete to land a college scholarship or even influence the admissions process is almost impossible. Therefore, parents need to be realistic about early success!"*

There are, of course, early bloomers who do continue on to be very successful in sports, partially as a result of some benefits of being an early bloomer that enhance their potential. To underscore this point: An interesting observation regarding the birth dates of professional soccer players was described in the best-selling book *Freakonomics* by Steven Levitt and Stephen J. Dubner. In that book, the authors pointed out that elite soccer players from the United States—and even moreso those from Europe—are more likely to have been born in the earlier months of the year than in the later months. They then go on to explain this "quirk" through the use of research on the subject of expert performance of athletes.

Specifically, the explanation is that USA and international soccer teams typically have a cutoff birth date, which is typically December 31. So when a coach is assessing two players in the same age bracket—one who happened to have been born in January and the other in December—the player born in January is likely to be bigger, stronger and more mature—and that player is more likely to be selected. And since that differentiation begins at a very young age in youth soccer, and most other sports, the January-born players are the ones who, *year after year*, receive the extra training, the attention, the practice and the positive feedback—along with the accompanying self-esteem and sports confidence. Thus, these athletes have a better chance of turning into elite athletes down the road.

Makes a lot of sense when you think about it, doesn't it?

If you are skeptical about this observation ... the same conclusions were developed through a separate research study by Canadian psychologist Roger Barnsley that showed:

> ✗ 40% of the young elite ice hockey players studied were born between: *January - March;*
>
> ✗ 30% were born between: *April – June;*
>
> ✗ 20% were born between: *July - September;*
>
> ✗ 10% were born between: *October – December.*

The independent researchers in both studies found that the children's athletic success was apparently more a result of special treatment and expectations—not necessarily their natural abilities.

On the other hand, there are also downsides to being an early bloomer:

- ✗ They don't have to work as hard and may eventually get passed up by those working harder.

- ✗ They have to live up to heightened expectations, which can lead to burnout from the pressure.

- ✗ They may define themselves by whether they win or lose, and their self-image becomes vulnerable because they are so young.

<u>LATE PHYSICAL AND/OR MENTAL DEVELOPMENT ... THOSE UNDERESTIMATED</u> *(LATE BLOOMERS)*

The stories of "late bloomers" have to be told, because there are just so many of them—and most kids, sports parents, and sports fans probably don't realize it. In fact, it is safe to say that there should be even more examples than there are, but many potential "late bloomers" probably give up before they should—out of discouragement, lack of support, and lack of confidence. They don't see the big picture and they don't have the perspective to believe they can succeed. In addition, they may not receive the support from parents, coaches, and other players.

This section is designed to perhaps keep some potential late bloomers motivated and supported a little longer. In fact, that, in itself, is one key goal of this book. Hopefully both parents and kids will understand, through real-world examples, that it is important to hang in there and work on developing and learning. Success can come later than expected. As sports psychologist Dr. Bob Rotella says, "You can't dictate when success occurs. Success comes to the person who does the right things repeatedly and patiently."

In spite of those athletes who might quit too early, there are many successful athletes who have looked past others' expectations. They used the fact that they were underestimated or overlooked as a tremendous motivator. Late bloomers are often successful simply because they had to work harder and longer than their "early bloomer" teammates, regardless of whether it was their physical or emotional development that was late in developing.

What makes the late bloomer athlete notable is that he/she didn't give up, when most others would have. As highly respected sports nutritionist Dave Ellis says, "Early bloomers have an advantage early on but are not as competitive once their competitors have matured. There is evidence that the athlete who didn't specialize early and was later in maturing might end up being the better athlete. These athletes are hungrier, they work harder and they have to be smarter players to make up for their size. And they end up with the tools and motivation to succeed instead of the burnout in ones who peaked too early."

One example: NBA star Dwyane Wade didn't see much playing time in high school until his junior year because his growth didn't kick in until the summer before that year—when he grew 4 inches. Even though he excelled after that, he still had to struggle, telling *Sports Illustrated Kids* that, "Nobody gave me a chance my rookie year. I had to work a lot harder to get the attention that I'm getting now. But it feels better this way."

Mark Tinordi had a 12-year career in the NHL, even though he was not drafted. And Adam Oates had a 19 year career in the NHL after initially signing as a free agent. (Oates is now a head coach in the NHL.)

Professional golfer Martin Piller could not make the starting five line-up on his college golf team, even as a senior. But he played in the Texas State Open after college and won enough money to allow him to try qualifying for the PGA. In his first try at Q-School he qualified for Nationwide Tour status and in his rookie year he had 3 top-10 finishes—ranking #7 on the Nationwide money list.

Following is a partial list of the many successful professional football players who went undrafted completely—and, in the end, proved everyone wrong:

Doug Baldwin	Kurt Warner
Victor Cruz	John Randle
Wes Welker	Rod Smith
Arian Foster	Warren Moon
London Fletcher	Priest Holmes
Tony Romo	Adam Vinatieri
Antonio Gates	Larry Little
James Harrison	Sam Mills

There are also those football players who initially went to the Canadian Football League ... and ultimately made their mark in the NFL, such as Warren Moon, Joe Theisman, and Jeff Garcia.

One player in particular—Anthony Calvillo—joined the Canadian Football League, stayed there, and went on to become football's all-time passing leader in 2011, while still playing in the CFL. Considered by most to be an "unlikely football star," Calvillo grew up in a difficult gang area of Los Angeles, and a friend of his even admits to jokingly ribbing Calvillo with, "Dude, you're poor. Your grades stink. You're just another Mexican kid from La Puente. Why would anyone think you could make it?"

Ryan Wolfe, the 5th player in college football to reach 300 receptions, only had one scholarship offer for college ... Nevada Las Vegas. As he told sportswriter Eric Sondheimer, "I used it as motivation to prove I was worthy of playing at the DI level and have people think twice. I've been working hard these last 4 years. It's not hard to turn a bad situation into a positive one."

Jack Perconte, former MLB player and youth sports expert, posted the following comment on his website, *baseballcoachingtips.net:* "Adversity is a great motivator. I will never forget a friend of mine laughing when I told him I wanted to be a major league player someday. I always tell kids that if every current major league player who was told they would never make it quit at that time, there would be a whole set of different big leaguers playing now."

Even though the NBA's Jeremy Lin led his high school team to a 32-1 record and a state title his senior year, and he was a finalist for Mr. Basketball State Player of the Year in 2006, he was ignored by Division I colleges. Some claimed that it was because of his Asian heritage, while others expressed concern that he lacked the necessary athleticism for college basketball; and his size was an issue because he was only 6'1" and 170 pounds when he graduated.

Lin went to Harvard and played basketball there, but was not drafted out of college. Floundering for a while in the NBA's developmental league, he was eventually given a chance in 2012 to start—and he showed what he could do on an NBA court (think: "Linsanity"). Said Lin in a "60 Minutes" interview, "It [not getting the attention] made me a stronger person."

In a *Yahoo!Sports* blog written by Frank Schwab, Eric Fisher is described as "one of the most unlikely first overall picks in NFL draft history." Nevertheless, he was drafted #1 in 2013. And this is how Schwab described Fisher: "Fisher was a two-star, unranked recruit [out of high school]. He was a skinny offensive tackle who had scholarship offers from Central Michigan and Eastern Michigan, and that's it." In fact, Fisher himself admits that he talked to Michigan State and Purdue about walking on, but "neither of them really wanted anything to do with me."

Schwab goes on to point out that even as recently as 2011, Fisher was just a third-team all-MAC selection as a junior and he failed to make even one first-team All-American squad as a senior; and that is why writer Schwab describes him as "the most unique first overall pick in NFL draft history."

Fisher sums up the whole experience with, "Hey, it doesn't matter where you start, it's where you end up. That's a big thing I take to heart."

Major League Baseball's Daniel Nava weighed 70 pounds his freshman year in high school and didn't play much baseball until his senior year. He then went to college at Santa Clara to play, but was still considered too small and was cut from the team—

and was made team manager. Not giving up, Nava transferred to a junior college. Then a growth spurt kicked in, so he returned to Santa Clara on a full scholarship and played well on the team. Nevertheless, he was not drafted by a Major League team and he ended up playing for an independent team—and was cut from that team.

Still not giving up, he went back to the same independent team the next year, played for them and was then signed by the Red Sox for $1.00. Posting great numbers in the minor leagues, he was called up to the majors—and then proceeded to hit a grand slam on the first major league pitch of his career!

In a *USA Today* interview, Nava's dad said, "I remember all the struggles. He was too small. He was too slow. People looked at his size rather than his heart. Every year he had written goals. He still does."

Eric Gagne, 2003 Cy Young Award winner, was not chosen in the baseball draft, and signed with the Dodgers as a free agent.

Darrell Armstrong ended his career with 11 seasons in the NBA, even though he was not drafted out of college and had to play 4 years in the developmental leagues and overseas.

A unique example of late blooming, from many years ago: The "pioneer of the jump shot," Paul Arizin, wasn't good enough at basketball to play for his high school team, so he played in local independent games. But according to the *Philadelphia Inquirer*, those independent games were played on slippery dance floors that weren't necessarily meant for basketball, and Arizin had difficulty getting his footing or setting his feet when making shots. To compensate for that difficulty, he started shooting with his feet off the floor—perfecting his "jump shot" out of necessity.

Arizin ended up going to Villanova for college, tried out for the basketball team there, and ended up with a stellar college and NBA career. In fact, he was eventually named College Player of the Year his senior year, and was ultimately elected to the NBA Hall of Fame.

Hard to believe, but ... famed quarterback Tom Brady was both underestimated and a late bloomer. He didn't even secure a full-time starting spot at the University of Michigan until halfway through his junior year, having to fight for the spot against Drew Henson. And Brady claims that it was that competition against Henson—a quarterback who was perceived to be better than Brady—that turned him into the superstar he became.

In an article about Brady's college experience, *Sports Illustrated* writer Michael Rosenberg makes the point that, "It wasn't until late in his college career that people began to form a picture of how good he would be. ... The Brady everybody sees today grew from the Brady nobody believed in at Michigan."

Even after college, however, Brady wasn't picked until the 6th round of the NFL draft (199th spot). Still underestimated after the draft, the *Boston Globe* described Brady as "a pocket passer who will compete for a practice squad spot." But Brady finally bloomed—and quickly led the Patriots to 3 Super Bowl victories before his 28th birthday.

Albert Pujols, the 2001 season Rookie of the Year, and now considered to be "one of the greatest baseball players of all time," wasn't drafted until the 13th round of the 1999 MLB draft—behind 401 other players. Though he came to the United States at the age of 16, speaking no English, he performed impressively through high school and community college, but didn't get much attention from the major league teams. And because he was big and strong (described as "a man among boys"), there were questions about his real age, and there were doubts about his long-term ability.

As reported in a *Los Angeles Times* column written by Mike DiGiovanna, one baseball scout recalled, "I didn't think he [Pujols] could play. First, there was his age. A lot of us thought he was older than he claimed." (The NCAA and MLB did eventually verify his birth certificate.) "He could really juice a fastball, but he couldn't handle the slider away. Plus, he was athletic, but not highly athletic. There was a question about what position he would play." Added the scout, "I missed, as a lot of scouts did, on his make-up and work ethic, ok?"

Referring to the draft day snub of Pujols, his community college coach, Marty Kilgore, said, "I don't think Albert has ever forgotten it."

Former NFL star Kurt Warner is a great "late bloomer" story, and is now considered to be one of the best undrafted players of all time. As an undrafted free agent after college in 1994, he tried out with the Green Bay Packers training camp, but was soon released. Disheartened, he went on to stock grocery shelves and eventually joined the Arena Football League. After a few years of showing what he could do in the AFL, he finally got the attention of the NFL and was signed. In the second string quarterback position behind the Rams' Trent Green, Warner got his start when Green was injured—and his performance resulted in "one of the top seasons by a quarterback in NFL history."

Hall of Fame pitcher Nolan Ryan showed impressive ability in high school, but most scouts were reportedly wary of his skinny body and limited control in pitching—so he didn't get a lot of attention. (He was 6'2" as a junior but weighed only 150 pounds.) Ryan was ultimately drafted—at 295th overall. Even when traded by the Mets in 1971 for Jim Fregosi, the Mets

General Manager told the *New York Times*, "As for Ryan, I really can't say I quit on him. But we've had him three full years and, although he's a hell of a prospect, he hasn't done it for us. How long can you wait? I can't rate him in the same category with Tom Seaver, Jerry Koosman or Gary Gentry." (It didn't take much longer for Ryan to show everyone what he could do.)

Professional basketball player Gilbert Arenas was 5'10" as a sophomore in high school, but eventually grew to 6'3". He described the effect of that height difference in *Sports Illustrated Kids*, saying that by being shorter than most of the other players his sophomore year he learned, "If your heart is bigger than the biggest guy on the team, then you're the biggest guy on the team."

For some late bloomers, it was being overweight that held them back.

Professional golfer Ricky Barnes weighed 225 pounds as a 14-year-old. Though he was a good athlete, he didn't have any speed or agility, so he worked at losing weight; and by the age of 15 he lost 65 pounds, simply by eating less and exercising more. He then became a very successful high school golfer and went on to win the US Amateur while still in college. Recognizing the impact of weight loss on his life, Barnes has since started the Ricky Barnes Foundation that supports youth golf programs and programs that are working against childhood obesity.

Mike Leake and Stephen Strasburg were young baseball teammates and they both went on to play professional baseball. But, as Leake told *USA Today*, Strasburg was "overweight, pouty and he used to cry" when he was 11. "He did a complete 180," said Leake.

According to the *USA Today* article, Strasburg, now considered to have been one of the greatest college pitchers of all time, had a very difficult freshman year at San Diego State. In fact, he reportedly came close to quitting baseball because he questioned himself. He was 25 pounds overweight, and never lifted weights, he was immature, and he was emotional and unable to handle adversity. He was in such bad shape that his strength and conditioning coach was quoted in the article as saying, "When I saw this guy and saw how out of shape and how unmotivated he was, I thought someone was playing a joke. This guy was throwing up every day we trained. I thought he had a medical condition, it was that bad. I finally told him 'You need to consider quitting. You're wasting your time.' "

Eventually Strasburg's pitching coach "got in his face and told him what people thought of him," which motivated Strasburg to get into the weight room, change his diet and lose weight. He also dedicated himself to working harder than anyone else on the team. Talking about that period, Strasburg has said, "People doubted me. People questioned my makeup. And I understand why they did. But there's such a difference in maturity now than when I was in high school, it's amazing."

Though it is generally assumed that height in basketball is nothing but an advantage, that is not always the case. One such story is that of Mark Eaton, former 7'4" NBA starting center for the Utah Jazz, and two-time NBA Defensive Player of the Year. Eaton was almost 7 feet tall as a teenager, but he "felt so small and insecure and shy," said filmmaker Stacy Dymalski in a *Los Angeles Times* article. As a result, Eaton had a very, very slow start to his basketball career."I was growing, I was un-coordinated, and I don't think the coaches knew what to do with me," explains Eaton.

With little apparent chance of playing basketball after high school, Eaton took a job at 18. However, he was eventually encouraged to give basketball another try by a coach who saw his potential, so he attended a junior college and then UCLA— eventually ending up in the starting line-up for the Utah Jazz for 10 years.

Finally ... though the legendary Michael Jordan was not a "late bloomer," this is a good opportunity to shed some reportedly factual light on the often repeated story that he was cut from his high school varsity team. Specifically ... Jordan *was* only 5'11" as a sophomore in high school, and it *is* true that he didn't play varsity basketball until his junior year (after he grew 4 inches in the summer), but he was the best *junior varsity* player on the team. As reported in the *Charlotte Observer*; Ruby Sutton, the physical education teacher at Jordan's high school, explains; "Back then, 10th graders played junior varsity; that's just the way it was. Nobody ever "cut" Michael Jordan.

Fred Lynch, the assistant basketball coach at the school during those years, does admit that the team made an exception to that rule during Jordan's sophomore year—sophomore Leroy Smith played on the varsity team. But, as Lynch explains, "Leroy was not a better basketball player than Mike, he just had size. We didn't have a lot of tall kids and Leroy was 6-6, 6-7 ... and [head coach] Pop Herring thought we had plenty of guards but needed size."

SUCCESSFUL ATHLETES THAT ARE RELATIVELY SMALL FOR THEIR SPORT

When Wayne Gretzky was asked at a press conference around the time of his induction into the Hockey Hall of Fame what he thought was the most significant contribution he made to the game of hockey, his answer was: *"I scored a victory for any player who is told he doesn't have the size, the strength, or the speed necessary to make an impact in the professional game."* He added, *"Growing up I was always the small guy. I couldn't beat people with my strength. My eyes and my mind have to do most of the work."*

There are a number of biographies of successful high school, college, and professional athletes whose relatively small size did not get in the way of them becoming successful athletes at their chosen sport. Based on their stories, what these "smaller" successful athletes came to realize very quickly was that their intense passion for a particular sport was just as important as their size. Their passion made them work harder on the skills that they were good at. Smaller athletes found a way to compensate for the perceived size disadvantage and developed different skills, and eventually their skills took them further than most people thought they could go.

One of the most common comments these athletes make in discussing their youth sports experiences and their success is, "When someone tells me I can't do something, it just makes me more determined to show them I can." (This goes along with the motivation of being underestimated, as discussed previously.)

I want to get this message to young athletes, so perhaps passing along some of the following stories will inspire a young athlete you, the adult reader, may know. Or, better yet ... just get your "smaller" young athlete to read this chapter himself/herself.

Just some of the professional football players under 5'9":

Stefan Logan - 5'6"
Darren Sproles - 5'6"
LaRod Stephens - 5'7"
Garrett Wolfe - 5'7"
Maurice Jones-Drew - 5'7"
Allen Rossum - 5'8"
Jason David - 5'8"
Michael Adams - 5'8"
Dantrell Savage - 5'8"
Tim Jennings - 5'8"
Sinorice Moss - 5'8"
Captain Munnerlyn - 5'8"
Jim Leonhard - 5'8"
Ray Rice - 5'8"

A few current and former NBA players under 6'0".........

Muggsy Bogues - 5'3"
Damon Stoudamire - 5'10"
Earl Boykins - 5'5"
Avery Johnson - 5'10"
Spud Webb - 5'7
Michael Adams - 5'10"   *(cont.)*

Greg Grant - 5'7"
Travis Best - 5'11"
Keith Jennings - 5'7"
Terrel Brandon - 5'11"
Allen Iverson - 5'11
Chucky Atkins - 5'11"
Speedy Claxton - 5"11"

NOTE: *According to "Sports Illustrated Teen," often the published heights for NBA players are even bumped up an inch or two.*

Even though major league baseball is a sport filled with statistics, the height and/or size of Major League Baseball players is not quite as significant an issue as it is in some other sports. Nevertheless, it might be interesting to note the following:

Baseball players on an *ESPN* list of "Best Short Players"...

Ivan Rodriguez
Dustin Pedroia
Miguel Tejada
Chuck Knoblauch
Tim Raines
Rafael Furcal
Kirby Puckett
Omar Vizquel
Jimmy Rollins
David Eckstein
Ray Durham
Tom Gordon

Sportswriter Eric Sondheimer wrote about two wrestlers who were also brothers, Anthony and Zahid Valencia. The brothers set a California state record by both winning state wrestling championships in their divisions during the same year, which was their freshman year. Most impressively, both also considered to be fairly small compared to their competitors. As their high school coach told Sondheimer, "They don't look like athletes at all, and I always tell them, 'That's to your benefit.' Everyone looks over and they think they can beat them. Everybody looks across the mat and says, 'That's the No. 1 guy in the state? OK, I'll beat that guy.' As the match progresses, you'll see their [Valencias'] conditioning kick in. They always wear everybody down and end up pinning most guys or pinning by technical fault."

Courtney Viney, once a UCLA cornerback at 5'8", was quoted in the *Los Angeles Times* as saying, "I love being 5'8". I love that teams will come after me. It gives me the chance to show I can play. Whenever I step on the field, I have something to prove." At the time, Viney's coach said of him:"He's not the biggest guy in the world, but you can't tell him that. That's why small players can play this game. They won't buy into the fact that they're small."

NBA player Earl Boykins, at 5'5", is said to excel by "doing everything very fast, with a quick release and a fast first step." Boykins himself has said that he "makes guys change the way they play, and that he has made his lack of height an advantage." (Boykins is the second shortest player in NBA history, behind Muggsy Bogues (5'3"). Said Boykins, in a *Sports Illustrated Teen* profile; "There is a pressure to play well because once you don't play well, the first thing they're going to say is 'He can't play because of his size.' If people just look at the height they don't understand basketball."

Playing at Baylor as one of the "best point guards in college," Odyssey Sims is only 5'8" tall. She has often explained, however, that she compensated for her lack of height, and worked on her skills when she was young by playing basketball against boys in order to get better.

Stefan Logan, a 5'6" NFL running back, played college football and set records at South Dakota; but because of his size he still had to prove himself in the Canadian Football League before the NFL would consider him. About size, Stefan was quoted in the *Los Angeles Times* as saying, "When you're smaller, a lot of people look down on you and think you can't get the job done because of your size. Some small guys come in and have a lot of confidence in themselves and are able to take on all challenges because they had to deal with it their whole life; he's not tall enough or he's too light."

According to some in the sports world ... "small guys" are becoming more popular in the NFL. *ESPN* analyst and former NFL coach Jon Gruden has explained that part of the reason for this is because of "more spread formations that allow skill position players to operate in open spaces rather than the more confined spaces of more traditional schemes. And a small running back can disappear behind a forest of offensive linemen."

Brothers James Rodgers and Jacquizz Rodgers were considered football stars in high school, but they were overlooked by most college recruiters because they were both considered too small at 5'7". However, they were fast and strong and the Oregon State coach recognized those qualities in them, and recruited them both. They quickly became two of the best college players in the nation. (Also note that it has also been said that they were the last to leave the practice field, and that they were always running extra sprints or playing games.)

The NFL's Darren Sproles, at 5'6" and 180 pounds, was a prominent player at Kansas State, and finished 5th in Heisman voting in 2003. But NFL scouts doubted him because of his size so he wasn't drafted until the 130th pick. He has since gone on to set records in the NFL.

NFL player Maurice Jones-Drew is relatively small for football at 5'7", and people often questioned his future in the game. But Jones-Drew responds to any doubts with, "You can't measure heart."

Dawn Staley is 5'6" and played professional basketball. Nevertheless, she claims that she was always told that she was too small, too short, and too slow to play basketball. However, described as "tough and determined," she excelled—becoming a two-time NCAA Player of the Year, a 5-time WNBA All-Star, and a 3-time Olympic Gold Medalist.

MLB superstar pitcher Tim Lincecum has been quoted as saying, "People have been doubting me my whole life." He was 4'11" and 85 pounds as a freshman in high school and only 5'9" and 135 by the time he was a freshman in college. But he says he excelled at baseball because "he could throw better than anyone," *in spite of his size.*

Superstar soccer player David Beckham was considered small for soccer when he was growing up, and was told at the ripe old age of 12 that he would never be able to play for England because of his size. But, according to a former coach, Beckham compensated for the size issue through very disciplined practice to develop a "free kick accuracy that other players wouldn't care about—and that became his primary strength."

NFL wide receiver Santana Moss, at 5'10", has often said that he was always small and was made fun of when he would proclaim that he wanted to be a wide receiver.

One of the smaller forwards in the NBA, Carlos Boozer, told *Sports Illustrated Kids*, "[When you're small] you have to be a little smarter because you can't just bully (big guys). They've got 3 or 4 inches on you. But you know what? If you've got passion and a desire to get something accomplished, you're going to be able to accomplish it. If you have passion, that's more impor- tant than any of those other things. You may be taller than me. You may even be more talented than me. But I've got more heart than you and more desire than you. I'm going to go out there and prove it."

In a poll of 313 major league players that was once conducted by *Sports Illustrated*, former MLB infielder David Eckstein, at only 5'7", was voted "the player who had gotten the most out of his talent." Eckstein was an All-Star, a World Series champion, and a World Series Most Valuable Player.

One of the best strikers in soccer history, Lionel Messi, is 5'7".

One of the more impressive "late-bloomer" stories is that of Clay Matthews III, Super Bowl winning linebacker for the Green Bay Packers. Matthews grew up in the legendary Matthews football family and he played high school football with a top private school football team in California. But he didn't start for the high school until his senior year, as he wasn't considered physically ready to play football until then. He was thought to be "too skinny, too weak, too slow."

Getting little college recruiting attention out of high school, Matthews walked on at USC in 2004 and red-shirted his freshman year. But even then, USC Coach Pete Carroll admitted to *USA Today* that he "thought it was intriguing. He [Matthews] had that big family background here. So I thought, 'OK, is there some magic in here somehow?' And I didn't see it. He looked like just a good, hard-working kid who was undersized, just not physically ready to match up." In fact, even Matthews admitted in the article that he didn't think his dad thought he would be where he ended up at USC.

Matthews developed his skills, body, and strength at USC, leading Coach Carroll to eventually admit that, "He does give hope to a lot of guys because he wasn't big enough and he wasn't fast enough ... but he is now. Now he's perfect."

Temeka Johnson, one of the WNBA's top point guards, is only 5'3".

Quarterback Drew Brees was considered too small and too skinny to be a college quarterback, and colleges were concerned that he had torn his ACL his junior year in high school. So, although he led his high school team to a 16-0 record his senior year, he was offered a scholarship by only 2 schools—Purdue and Kentucky. He chose Purdue because Kentucky already had a star quarterback.

After having been ignored by Texas A & M, the college where he originally had hoped to play, Brees later told *Sports Illustrated*, "I won't forget the people who thought I couldn't succeed, but this [Purdue] is the right place for me." (Following his stellar college performance, Brees was drafted by the NFL in the second round ... and the rest is history.)

Four-time NBA Defensive Player of the Year, Ben Wallace, played at Division II Virginia Union and signed as a free agent, because he was not drafted out of college. He was dismissed because of his lack of size. As one scout explained in *Sports Illustrated Teen*, "Most people thought he [Wallace] was not tall enough to be a center and not skilled enough to be an effective forward. As it turns out, we put too much emphasis on his lack of size and not enough on his strength, his work ethic and his unbelievable ability to rebound the ball."

IS IT MENTAL?

According to behavioral research discussed in an article on StrengthPlanet.com, the psychological profiles of world class/elite athletes include <u>low scores</u> in tension, depression, anger, fatigue, and confusion; and <u>high scores</u> in self confidence, mental toughness, and determination. The research also indicates that elite athletes' psychological profiles are very different from those of both non-elite athletes and the normal population, overall. Non-elite athletes' profiles are more similar to the profiles of non-athletes and the normal population, in general.

Books, magazines, research articles and psychologists endlessly take part in the analysis of the "mind of an athlete," and there are just as many perspectives about the mental side of sports as there are books and experts. Therefore, this chapter will just get you started on the topic, and will provide references for how to explore the topic further.

One example of the relationship between physical and mental abilities in athletes: NFL defensive tackle Ndamukong Suh started playing football his sophomore year in high school and played at the University of Nebraska, but he had what was described as a "fairly lackluster college career." In an interview with *Sports Ilustrated,* Suh described his early frustration because it seemed that "something was missing" from his game— so he turned to his defensive coordinator for guidance.

According to the team's defensive coordinator, Carl Pelini, Suh was big, strong and talented, but the "mental aspect of his game was missing." Suh was fairly quiet and shy, so he had to learn how to "leave his personality at home and had to stop avoiding contact." With that goal in mind, Pelini made Suh go through mental repetitions during practice, and Suh came to understand the process and benefit from it. Says Suh, "You watch and learn from someone else's mistakes. It opened my eyes to a whole new side, the mental side of the game."

Suh eventually became the nation's leading defensive lineman in tackles, tackles for loss, and sacks. (Maybe he went overboard in his transformation ... he now is often described as a "dirty player.")

Every sport requires mental skills, but perhaps no sport requires more mental control than golf. As golf psychologist/guru Dr. Joseph Parent explained in a *FORE* magazine article, "No matter how sophisticated their equipment or knowledge of the swing, if golfers don't know how to work their minds on the course, they encounter the common mental obstacles that keep them from realizing their potential."

SPORTS INTELLIGENCE

"Sports Intelligence" is often given the credit for some of the success of certain elite athletes, and sports intelligence is also given credit for "making up for" physical or skill shortcomings in successful athletes. But what's most interesting about this quality is the different ways this form of intelligence is depicted.

One example of an athlete who is considered to be quite "smart" in his sport is NBA player Chris Bosh, who has been described as "very analytical" about how his body works. He is also described as a fast learner who watched professional athletes while he was growing up and absorbed much of what he observed. In addition, NBA coach Sam Mitchell has been quoted as saying that Bosh "is coachable, he listens to things you tell him."

LeBron James reportedly has an extra level of "basketball intelligence" in his game. According to comments made to *Sports Illustrated Kids* by James' former guardian and coach, Frankie Walker, Sr.; "What really made LeBron stand out from the other kids playing the game was how quickly he learned to 'think basketball.' He began to approach the game of basketball the way a chess master approaches chess. LeBron had the ability to see ahead. I had never coached a kid who picked up things and excelled in them as quickly as LeBron."

Football quarterbacks are generally thought of as being intelligent, and much of that intelligence is, of course, "sports intelligence." Ravens' quarterback Joe Flacco was described by his quarterback coach in a *Baltimore Sun* interview this way: "He's like a sponge. If you tell him something, he has the ability to switch his thinking and move on to the next step ... He's a guy that can process information very quickly, recalculate it in his mind, and then go and make the proper decision."

Superstar Peyton Manning is said to have a type of "photographic memory" when it comes to remembering plays from previous games—even games from several years back—and he endlessly studies details on game tapes.

And said quarterback Colin Kaepernick in a *GQ* interview: "I think the biggest part of my game that's underestimated is the mental part of it. Probably because it's invisible. You can't see the hours I put in."

In addition to his athletic ability, Josh Hamilton was also described in a *SportsIllustrated.com* article by a former coach as "understanding the mechanics of the game, even as a teenager." Said the coach, "He would talk to me about bat speed, his hip rotation, his weight shift ..."

NBA player Chris Bosh has often been described as "very smart, a fast learner, he is very analytical about how his body works, and is astutely observant of how the game of basketball is played." In fact Bosh, himself, has explained that he developed his skills, in part, by closely observing the games and moves of professional basket- ball players while he was growing up.

After pro baseball's Jerry Sands was called up to the majors by the Dodgers, General Manager Ned Colletti made this comment about Sands: "He's got an ability to read a situation, to slow it down in his mind."

FIELD SENSE

Another aspect of "natural talent" that is often discussed by sports experts and athletes is the concept of "field sense"— described as a mixture of anticipation, timing, and an acute sense of spacial relations. According to an article that examines the idea of "field sense" (written by Jennifer Kahn for *Wired Magazine*), this concept of a natural "field sense" has long been assumed to be innate—you either have it or you don't. But the *Wired* article goes on to discuss that Peter Vint, a researcher who specifically studies "field sense," rejects the notion that it can't be learned, and he clearly believes that "perceptual ability (field sense) develops, in part, to help a physical underdog against bigger, stronger players." In other words ... "If you can anticipate a throw, you don't have to be as fast." Adds Vint, "In any sport, you come across these players [with field sense]. They're not always the most physically talented, but they're by far the best. The way they see things that nobody else sees—it can seem almost supernatural."

Vint also uses the term "psychic plays," describing an athlete's "ability to calculate the movements of every person on the field, or to time a pass so perfectly that the receiver doesn't even break stride."

Another researcher who provides insight in the same *Wired* article is Damian Farrow. In his research, Farrow claims to have determined that field sense can, indeed, be learned, but that "it has to be an unconscious process of learning in order for it to work." Having studied the youth sports activities of successful athletes, Farrow believes that many athletes naturally develop a field sense through backyard games or unstructured play— play that fosters flexible thinking and acute spatial attention. In fact, as a result of his findings, Farrow points out that "society should be encouraging more of this type of activity [unstructured play], as opposed to ever more structured physical activities and sports for our youth."

Wayne Gretzky, for one, has been described as possessing a "natural field sense." Said one opponent of Gretzky's, "I'd see him [Gretzky] come down the ice and immediately start thinking 'What don't I see that Wayne's seeing right now?' " (Gretzky believes that his field sense developed naturally as compensation for his relatively smaller size.)

Similar to "field sense" is the concept of "football awareness" that former USC football coach Lane Kiffin described in a *Los Angeles Times* article as being "what takes over in a game situation. It's understanding angles, but also adjusting on the fly." Kiffin went on to explain that "football awareness is the most difficult thing to evaluate. Pro scouts often misjudge first-round picks because they put too much emphasis on size and 40-yard dash times." (Star quarterback Joe Montana, among others, was said to have this special, acute sense of everything that was going on around him on the football field.)

ABILITY TO WITHSTAND PRESSURE

Successful athletes who are confident and have a significant competitive streak also tend to thrive under pressure. For example, the NBA's Jeremy Lin is said to be "at his best under pressure," and as Lin's former AAU coach has said, "For Jeremy, its always been that he glows—he just glows—when he's in the spotlight. It's just his make-up. It's his determination to succeed."

An athlete's ability to withstand pressure also depends, in large part, on the ability to focus on the immediate play at hand, without thinking about what the play means "in the big picture."

A good example of this is former Stanford quarterback Tavita Pritchard, who led his team during the huge upset game in which Stanford beat their arch-rival USC in 2007. Pritchard only found out 6 days before that game that he would be the starting quarterback, having never started a Stanford game before—and having no collegiate touchdown passes, and only one collegiate completion. That's incredible pressure, regardless of the opponent. But for it to be against USC ...

After the Stanford win, Pritchard explained his thoughts regarding the final 11 minutes of the game: "If I thought about it, I never would have been able to do it. But because I was so new, I didn't have time to think, I was too busy just trying to call the right plays."

When asked how he prepares for a big game, pro baseball's Dontrelle Willis told *Sports Illustrated Kids,* "I prepare the same way I prepared for a game in high school. I try to stay loose and keep telling myself it's 'just a ball game.' You just have to remember it's still 60 feet, 6 inches [between the pitching rubber and home plate] no matter how many people are there."

Some athletes who handle pressure well are those who can take their play very seriously, but also have a lot of fun when they are playing. NFL quarterback Kirk Cousins describes Robert Griffin III as one of those athletes. Said Cousins to *Yahoo!Sports* writer Les Carpenter; "What I've learned from Robert is to have fun and enjoy it. He didn't look like he was carrying the weight of the world on his shoulders even though he had every right to. You don't have to be serious to be a great leader."

Baseball superstar Derek Jeter is said to be another one of those athletes that has fun during the game, even chatting with fans while in the on-deck circle. As he once told *ESPNNewYork.com,*

"The bigger the situation, the more the game speeds up. That's all mental. It messes people up. You think, I've got to do this, I've got to do that' when in reality all you have to do is the same thing you've always been doing. Slow it down. Realize you've been in this situation before. You've been successful in this situation before. Be calm. The more you can do that, the more pressure you take off yourself and the easier it is to perform."

After moving to the Yankees, pitcher Mike Mussina was often asked about the increased pressure of playing for the legendary New York team, and he would tell anyone who asked that it didn't matter to him which stadium he played in because he was "just pitching." In one particular interview he did explain that he grew up practicing pitching at a strike zone painted on his barn, where he would imagine he was pitching "somewhere else." So when he got to the big leagues, he just started imagining that he was pitching to the strike zone on his barn—*no matter who he was pitching for, or against.*

Sadly, there are athletes who have great drive, a strong love of the game, and tremendous athletic skills, but they have difficulty handling the pressure and stress that come with high level competitive sports. One such example is professional tennis player Rebecca Marino, who was once ranked as high as 38th in the world in women's professional tennis. But she retired from the game at the age of 22 "because she was struggling with all the online abuse she was getting from fans that berated her on social media." She also acknowledged that she had battled depression for several years and that tennis wasn't fun for her anymore.

In a column about Marino's retirement that appeared on *Yahoo!Sports*, Shane Bacon wrote, "... while some people can brush it off, there is a large group of people that see that stuff and have a hard time looking past it. Imagine if you just lost some big match and the first thing you see is people scolding you and telling you to die? Sadly, this is the world we live in."

Some very successful professional athletes do have temporary stages where they react to the pressure of the sport, or to the media, or whatever else might be going on in their lives. Even the great pitcher Stephen Strasburg experienced such a stage of pressure when he was taken out of commission in 2012 as part of a plan to limit his innings pitched in the season. It was an emotional time for Strasburg, but his manager, Davey Johnson, explained, "If you're not there 100 percent mentally ... I don't see the crispness. I don't see the ball jumping out of his hand." Johnson added, "*I'm a firm believer that this game's 90 – 95 percent mental and he's [Strasburg] only human.* I don't know how anybody can be totally mentally concentrating on the job at hand with the media hype to this thing, and I think we'd be risking more by sending him out."

ABILITY TO FOCUS

Sports psychologists often say that athletes who think too much make mistakes. "The very best athletes put themselves in a bubble, just focus on the moment and let their bodies do what they have trained to do without letting their minds get in the way," says sports psychiatrist Ronald Kamm. "At the very top level that's the difference between the winners and the also-rans." In the words of Dr. Joseph Parent, golf psychologist and noted author of the book *Zen Golf: Mastering the Mental Game*:

"When body and mind are synchronized in the present moment, we can uncover our inherent dignity and confidence."

Drew Brees's Purdue football coach, Joe Tiller, once said of Brees; "He [Brees] does something that very good quarterbacks and good athletes do that probably 90% of the people who compete in intercollegiate athletics don't do. When he makes a mistake, he has the ability to focus on the next opportunity versus dwelling on the past mistake."

Golfer Rickie Fowler, the youngest PGA Tour member in 2010, talked to *Golf.com* about his style of play, in which he plays faster than most golfers. Described as a "real daredevil on the course," Fowler said, "It's like doing a big jump. You can't sit there and think about it for too long or else you're going to start thinking about all the bad things that could happen. You just go do it. And that's what I've done with golf—step up, look at the shot, get the number and go."

Knuckleball phenom R.A. Dickey told the *Los Angeles Times,* "The only goal I set at the start of the season was to throw my very first pitch as well as I can throw it. My next goal was to throw the second pitch as well as I can throw it. The final result will be an overflow of the commitment to the moment."

The father of NFL quarterback Colin Kaepernick told *Fox40* television reporter Luana Munoz that one of Colin's unique traits is the "ability to focus." Explained Rick Kaepernick: [Colin has the ability] "to put things that are on the outside, on the outside, and basically say 'I have a job to do here. I am quarterback for the San Francisco 49ers. I owe it to the coaches. I owe it to my teammates and I owe it to my fans. I have to do a job.' "

Michael Jordan was particularly well-known for his ability to focus during a basketball game—even when he was on the bench. A story has been told that when a young fan asked him what he thought about during a time out, his response was that he "just thinks about chewing his gum."

Record-setting hurdler Johnathan Cabral put his ability and need to focus into words for the *Ventura County Star:* "Mentally, up to the race, you just have to be in your zone. You have to relax; you can't be all tense. Then five minutes before your race you just switch over your mindset. You go into your serious mode."

Another element of focus requires that an athlete focus only on the immediate task at hand, and not focus on specific statistics, scores and championships. In fact, you will often hear professional athletes claim that they don't pay attention to the score of a game. Said MLB player Ryan Braun, when asked about his statistics during his stellar rookie year; "My family and friends know my stats more than I do. I'll look at that stuff at the end of the season."

Finally ... In one of his many "profound quips," the legendary Yogi Berra described what he would think about when he was playing well: "Gee, when I'm concentrating and playing real good, I can't think." (Is there a better description of focus?)

PASSION ... DREAMS ... GOALS

Dr. Anders Ericsson is a psychologist devoted to studying what it is that makes people extraordinarily good at something, and he claims that research supports the idea of needing to "love what you do" to be good at it. As stated by Dr. Ericsson in the book *Freakonomics*: "You should do what you love, because if you don't love it, you are unlikely to work hard enough to get very good."

However, there is a significant difference between "liking something a lot" and "loving something"—and some young athletes may mistakenly consider their "extreme like" for a sport to be "love".

Passion for a sport can develop over time or it can occur early on in a sports experience. For example, NBA great Dwyane Wade claims he didn't even really like basketball at first, preferring baseball and football. But after his dad took him to a basketball court for a solid week he "fell in love with the game." Wade says that, after that, "he didn't have to make me play; he had to stop me from playing."

Amy Anderson, the 2009 U.S. Girls Junior Golf Champion, told *Sports Illustrated* that her dad never had to tell her to practice. Said Amy, "I loved spending hours on the range." She also told how other parents want to know how to get their kids to practice that much, and she simply tells them, "I worked so hard because I loved the game and wanted to win."

The sister of WNBA star Diana Taurasi has said that "Diana was born with a ball in her hand. As kids, we'd spend hours and hours practicing our free throws. There was nothing else she'd rather do."

The reverse of all of this, however, is that an athlete might stop playing their sport when they lose their passion—*in spite* of their ability or the money or a professional opportunity—and there are those that have done that, as well. Take Aaron Curry, considered one of the best NFL prospects when drafted 4th overall. But four years later, after a very disappointing performance in the pros, he left football because he realized that he no longer had the passion for the game. Said Curry, in explaining his quick descent; "I knew I could do it. I knew I would do it. At the time, I wasn't motivated to do it. Football wasn't my top priority, to be honest."

On the other hand ... there are successful athletes who admit that they are not necessarily passionate about the particular sport that they are playing, but are, instead, passionate about competition, excelling, achieving a goal, or being the best they can be and improving— regardless of which sport they play. In fact, athletes will sometimes even admit that they prefer a different sport than the one they are playing. But, going back to the concept of multiple sport athletes, this is how they are able to excel at more than one sport. They don't have to be playing their favorite sport, but they have to be passionate about an element of athletic participation that inspires them.

Successful athletes also often talk in terms of their "dream" of playing sports professionally. One example: Roberto Garza, Jr., one of the few Latinos in the NFL, says his desire to play in the NFL started at a very young age—regardless of the fact that he had no encouragement. In fact, it has also been said that he had no reason to believe that he could ever play professional football, having been reminded frequently that "Latinos don't play football." His mother, however, was quoted in a *Los Angeles Times* article as saying, "He [Garza] had this very clear dream that nobody else had, nobody else understood. Every time I'm awake I see him working on this dream. He believed even when nobody else did."

In his Hall of Fame speech, baseball's Rickey Henderson told kids: "To all the kids out there, follow your dreams, believe in your dreams, because dreams do come true."

NFL running back Arian Foster told sportswriter Sam Farmer that when he was 16, his high school teacher asked each kid in class what they wanted to do when they grow up. Said Foster, "I told the teacher I wanted to be in the NFL. She kind of laughed and asked me 'what else' I wanted to do. I was kind of offended because ... I was the only one that was asked 'what else' I wanted to do." Added Foster's father, Carl; "We've always encouraged all of our kids to pursue their hopes and dreams. You can't really listen to other people. You've got to kind of blank them out."

Finally ... in his Football Hall of Fame speech, the great running back Emmitt Smith talked about his dream of playing football. Said Smith, "There's a difference between merely having a dream and fulfilling a vision. Most people only dream. I not only had my childhood dream, but I did everything in my power to fulfill it. I wrote down my goals and how I was going to achieve them because Dwight Thomas [Smith's high school coach] used to tell us, 'It's only a dream until you write it down, and then it becomes a goal.' " Added Smith, "I began to feed the dream with my passion and dedication. I loved the sport so much, all I wanted to do was just play it. It didn't matter to me what position I played. I just loved being out there."

CONFIDENCE ... COURAGE ... NOT AFRAID TO MAKE A MISTAKE

The questions parents want answered are:

How is sports confidence developed?

How much influence do parents and coaches have on it?

Does it go hand-in-hand with confidence in other areas of life, or is confidence in sports different?

Does a child have to be an excellent athlete to feel confident?

What if a child lacks confidence in their athletic ability?

There are several expert resources listed in the Appendix to this book that will address those questions in detail. Sports psychologists spend half their time on this very topic. But, following are many comments made by successful athletes that provide insight, as well:

"CONFIDENCE IS WHAT HAPPENS WHEN YOU'VE DONE THE HARD WORK TO SUCCEED."
(Too many coaches and psychologists have been quoted saying this to attribute it to any one person.)

Major League Baseball player Brett Gardner went to walk-on tryouts at the College of Charleston, and (confidently) went back to the field to practice before he was notified whether he made the team or not. Since he was there, the coach let him practice with the team, but he was warned that he would have to leave if he didn't hold up. Gardner ended up being a 3-year starter for the team, he was drafted in the third round of the 2005 MLB draft after his junior year, and he made it to the majors by 2008. Gardner has often explained that he knew he was capable of playing Division I baseball and just needed the chance to prove it.

In his Hall of Fame speech, NFL tight end Shannon Sharpe explained, "When people told me I'd never make it, I listened to the one person who said I could: me."

Major League pitcher Mike Leake (drafted 8th overall) has the word "Believe" tattooed over the right side of his rib cage, and has been quoted as saying, "I always thought I could do it, even if nobody else did. I just have some weird inner confidence that gets me going."

By all accounts, NFL star Clay Matthews III had no reason to "feel confident" that he could succeed in the USC football program—let alone even get on the team—after having only a moderately impressive high school performance record, and after only being recruited by community colleges. But Matthews *did* have confidence, and it worked for him; and he *did* walk on at USC his freshman year. Said Matthews, himself, about walking on: "I knew I was capable of playing with the best athletes in the nation. I thought I could come in here, day one, and be the guy. Maybe I was crazy to have that mind-set, but obviously that's better than saying you can't."

In a *Baltimore Sun* interview, the quarterback coach of the Baltimore Ravens described Joe Flacco's self- confidence: "The scout's first impression was that he was calm. There was a certain confidence he has in his eyes that's hard to explain. He carries himself very confidently, but not arrogant or cocky."

Olympic soccer star Mia Hamm told *USA Today* that she thinks that courage is a key trait that sets successful athletes apart from the others. Using an example to clarify her thought, she explained, "It takes great skill for Tiger to hit a 2-iron 260 yards over the water. But it also takes courage to go for that shot. He doesn't think about failure. That's what's so impressive."

BleacherReport.com sportswriter Zach Pumerantz wrote, "[Brett] Favre believed he could make every throw, fit the pigskin in between every defender—and 336 times he was wrong." Nevertheless, Favre goes down as one of the greatest quarterbacks of all time.

Stanford football coach David Shaw told *Yahoo!Sports* that confidence is one of the most important attributes he looks for when recruiting for the Stanford team. As Shaw explained, "We seek a young man that has the confidence to stand up in front of you and express himself, as opposed to what a lot of young kids do today; they don't give you eye contact, they kind of mumble when they talk to adults." He added, "We play that way. We are going to play right at you, in your face, 'Here is who we are, here is how we play.' There is a one-to-one correlation. There is no doubt about it to me. The inability to be intimidated by a person or a situation is something that is significant."

Sportswriter Ian Thomsen had an insightful reaction to NBA basketball's Kemba Walker being drafted by the Bobcats in 2011: "It was initially surprising that the Bobcats invested the #9 pick in another small guard ... after being frustrated at the time by 6-foot incumbent D.J. Augustin. But they [Walker and Augustin] couldn't be more different: While Augustin undervalues his own talent and doesn't give himself enough credit, Walker flows over with confidence. He believes he should succeed because no one is better, and that's the first step to thriving in the NBA."

Is it possible for an athlete to be overly confident? Some in the press consider baseball's Josh Beckett to be just that—describing him as "cocky, arrogant, brash," etc. In fact, his cockiness supposedly kept him from being drafted #1 overall. But, explains Beckett, "I'm confident in myself, either way. I've pitched big games all my life." And, said former Marlins manager Jack McKeon, "One thing about him [Beckett]; he may talk a lot, but he walks the walk, as well."

It's not unusual, though, for "over-confident" athletes to be brought down to earth eventually—particularly if they can't live up to their self-image. Friends, teammates, and coaches are usually good at cutting them down to size quickly, even at a young age. (See section on humility.)

On the other hand, it is important to note that sometimes it is actually a *lack of confidence* that acts as a motivator for young athletes—particularly if it results in them endlessly practicing because they don't think they are good enough. There are successful athletes who claim that it was, indeed, a lack of confidence that kept them working as hard as they did at their sport.

Recently retired pro baseball player Andy Pettitte was named Houston High School Player of the Year, but his mother has been quoted as saying that, "Andy sometimes lacked confidence and he worked so hard but he never thought it was good enough." In Andy's mind "it was always the other guy who was awesome." His mom said she would just tell him, "Keep on working. Don't give up," when he would express these thoughts.

NBA star Blake Griffin told the *Los Angeles Times*, "The mentality when I was younger was I wasn't as skilled as everybody else. So I had to outwork them. I had to put in the work and had to do all this stuff. And that has to be your mentality the whole time."

Star quarterback Tom Brady told *Sports Illustrated Kids*: "I've never been very big or very strong or very fast. Because of that, there's always insecurities that I have." He went on to explain that he has always used those insecurities to work harder and reach higher goals.

It is also important for young kids and teens, as well, to understand that no athlete is confident 100% of the time. Anyone can be subject to "bouts of doubts" about their abilities, their futures, their commitment; but it is how they process those doubts that makes the difference. For example, when *SIKids.com* asked baseball superstar Mark Teixeira if he ever thought he wasn't good enough to play in the major leagues, he answered, "Always. Baseball is a very hard sport and there is always doubt that creeps into your mind. But I tried to have a positive attitude and work hard."

Heisman winner Matt Leinart told *SIKids.com* that he wasn't sure he was good enough to win the quarterback position over the other three candidates when he was at USC. Explained Leinart, "I had some doubts about what I could do. But then I realized that if you don't believe in yourself, how can anyone else believe in you? There was no way I was going to be the starting quarterback unless I was convinced I could do it."

After winning the position, and following a 12-1 season, Leinart was described by his coach, Pete Carroll: "Matt has turned into a terrific quarterback in a short time. I think part of it is he's a fast learner. The other part is due to his confidence. Ever since he became the starter, I've never seen him look unsure of himself." Leinart's advice to young athletes: "It's OK to have doubts. Everyone has doubts. But if you want to be a success at anything, you have to put those doubts aside. If you have confidence in yourself, when your opportunity comes, you'll be ready to jump on it."

In a *Sports Illustrated Kids* interview, NFL quarterback Aaron Rodgers talked candidly about how he felt when he took over the quarterback position after Brett Favre. "I had a lot of confidence in my abilities. But the doubts and worries were associated with 'How am I going to be perceived by my teammates? How's my performance going to be scrutinized?' In the back of your mind, that negative voice is telling you ... 'You're not as good as you think you are.' Those can mess with you a little bit, but you can also draw some motivation from those negative thoughts, and I did."

Finally ... in my humble opinion, there is no quote about confidence that is more clever than that of legendary former football coach Barry Switzer, who once famously said; *"SOME PEOPLE ARE BORN ON THIRD BASE AND GO THROUGH LIFE THINKING THEY HIT A TRIPLE."* (Think about it ...)

PERSEVERANCE ... PATIENCE ... MENTAL TOUGHNESS ... RESILIENCE

MANY OF LIFE'S FAILURES ARE PEOPLE WHO DID NOT REALIZE HOW CLOSE THEY WERE TO SUCCESS WHEN THEY GAVE UP.
— Thomas Edison

THE DIFFERENCE BETWEEN A SUCCESSFUL PERSON AND OTHERS IS NOT A LACK OF STRENGTH, NOT A LACK OF KNOWLEDGE, BUT RATHER IN A LACK OF WILL.
—Vince Lombardi

Young athletes will have difficult games, streaks of poor performance, and even difficult years. And, starting at a very young age, children participating in organized sports will all get some form of negative input from coaches, peers/teammates, parents, etc. It's inevitable. Some can handle all of it better than others.

The difference between athletes who bounce back quickly and successfully after negative experiences, and those who end up falling apart is that some athletes have more resilience and/or perseverance than others.

Looked at in a slightly different way: those that persevere at least have a chance of success ... and those that don't persevere will never know what might have happened if they hadn't quit. There is no doubt that many would-be, future high school, college and professional athletes give up too soon. Consider this book's section on "Late Bloomers" (which overlaps this topic).

Most of those who succeeded a little later than others succeeded only because they didn't give up— when many would have.

It is very important that kids learn about perseverance at a young age. They need to understand that a poor performance, a negative review, or an injury is NOT the end of the world or the end of athletic achievement—though it might seem like it to them at the time. Perhaps the following examples will help provide perspective:

Psychologist Angela Duckworth told *Psychology Today* that she believes that "passion can foster perseverance," but that "perseverence can foster passion, as well." One example of this notion is found in the childhood of WNBA star Kaleena Mosqueda-Lewis, as described by *ESPNW*. Mosqueda-Lewis started playing basketball in third grade, didn't really like it, and wasn't very good at it. In fact, she was cut from her basketball team. So her dad said to her, "If this is something you really want to do and you don't want to feel like this again we can make that happen." "So," explains Mosqueda-Lewis,"every day from then on I practiced with my dad at the gym and that's where I knew that basketball is what I want to do forever."

According to a *Psychology Today* article about perseverance that was written by Peter Doskoch, some psychologists refer to the concept of perseverance as "grit"—*the determination to accomplish an ambitious, long-term goal despite the inevitable obstacles*. And there is no greater test of an athlete's "grit" than what he/she needs to do to successfully come back from an injury. Some athletes fail this test, while others make it.

One example of grit: Heisman winner and #2 NFL draft pick Robert Griffin III exhibited perseverance and resilience when he was in college and experienced a torn ACL during the third game of his sophomore year at Baylor. Griffin's father was quoted in a *YahooSports.com* article as saying, "Robert was very determined not to let the injury beat him, but it is hard when you feel there is no one who understands what you are feeling—the pain, the disappointment, wondering what the future holds for you."

Working with former track star and Houston track coach Leroy Burrell, who had once successfully come back from a similar injury, Griffin did just what he had to do—though it wasn't easy and it wasn't necessarily a sure thing. Said Burrell, "I said there would be times when he [Griffin] would wonder whether it was worth all the effort it would take to get back there. I wanted him to realize that the rewards were worth that struggle, that he had to go in fully and make it back." And make it back, he did.

It also takes resilience and perseverance to survive rejection in sports. In a column discussing the frustration of a few excellent high school athletes who were overlooked by colleges, sportswriter Eric Sondheimer wrote, "Unfortunately, there are lots of successful high school players who go unnoticed or unappreciated by college recruiters. People can place blame on lack of exposure or failure to impress at camps or combines, but the bottom line is football recruiters know what they want, and if you don't fit into their mold, it will create obstacles to reaching the next level. Perhaps those who didn't sign letters will get a chance to play after enrolling at a college as a walk on or making it through the junior college ranks. It's frustrating, but opportunities come to those who don't give up."

It takes tremendous resilience to fight through rejection during any level of team selection/drafting/recruiting and to keep going:

some can do it and some can't. Even the NFL's star quarterback Aaron Rodgers had to develop this perseverance in his younger years, as he received only one offer from a Division I college after high school—as a walk on. Though he had a strong high school football record, the Division I schools thought he was too small (5'10"). Discouraged, Rodgers considered giving up football completely, but ended up going to a community college and worked hard to show what he could do there. He ultimately played for Cal Berkeley, set records, and was drafted in the first round of the NFL draft.

Nevertheless, Rodgers *still* had to persevere and be patient, as he was back-up to legend Brett Favre for three years before he got his chance to shine. Said Rodgers to *Sports Illustrated Kids*, "It's something that gives me perspective all the time, knowing that the road I took was difficult. But it did shape my character and it shaped my games as well ... It took a lot to get where I am now and it's going to take a lot to stay where I'm at."

Some fans may not realize that R.A. Dickey, one of the most dominating pitchers of the 2012 and 2013 Major League Baseball seasons, spent nearly a decade as a "journeyman pitcher"—until he worked intensely to develop the knuckleball so that he would be able to throw it full-time.

Dickey was originally a first round draft pick, but it was later discovered that he was missing a ligament in his throwing elbow and that limited his perceived value to the team. That's when he decided to make the transition to being the only major league player in 2012 throwing the knuckleball. He persevered, and adapted to a potentially career-limiting change in circumstances.

Hiroki Kuroda, starting pitcher for the Dodgers, reportedly spent most of his high school baseball career on the bench and was said to be the "third-best pitcher" on his high school team in

Japan. In fact, his high school coach told the *Los Angeles Times* that he "never imagined he [Kuroda] would be able to pitch [for the Dodgers]. Pro scouts frequently came to watch our teams play, but no one bothered with Kuroda. There was no point."

Kuroda admitted that he considered giving up baseball when he graduated from high school, but he felt like he "hadn't done everything I could." So he tried out for his college baseball team, gradually improved his skills, and was eventually drafted by Major League Baseball in the United States. Kuroda told the *Los Angeles Times* that he hopes his story can inspire late-developing players. "Right now, I'm sure there are many kids out there who want to quit," he said. "High school was really tough for me, but I think those bad times were beneficial to me. No matter what happens, I know I can deal with it."

Patrick Roy, one of the best NHL goal tenders ever, told *Kukla's Korner*, "There were situations when I was younger, it would have been very easy for me to do something else. I was cut when I was a Midget from Double C. I decided to persevere ... and the following year I made the AAA. It's obvious that a lot of things might not have happened if I didn't persevere."

Considering the need for patience in athletic development, Matt Holiday, a highly regarded power hitter in pro baseball, was quoted in an article by Matt Smith at *mlb.com* as saying that he had to learn "to hit for average before focusing on hitting home runs." He explained; "As a young player, it's important to use the whole field. That's important in the maturation of a hitter. As you learn to hit the ball the opposite way, you understand when you can try and pull the ball for a home run. I learned to hit the ball the other way first." He added, "I had some tough times. Now that I look back on it, I'm very grateful for those times. I know now that I needed them. But at the time you think, 'Man I wish I could just get to the major leagues.' "

In a sport such as golf, it sometimes takes incredible perseverance and patience to keep going—tournament after tournament, without a win. Unlike professional team sports, there is no one to tell you you're on or off the team. There is always another golf tournament to enter, whether you're winning or losing. So sometimes golfers are able to persevere even longer than other athletes, and sometimes that extreme perseverance pays off. For example, golfer Harrison Frazar won his *first* PGA Tour title in his 355th tournament, a month before he turned 40. (What if he had quit golf after the 354th consecutive tournament he didn't win?)

Major League catcher Stephen Vogt played baseball at Azusa Pacific, an NAIA school, and was passed over in the 2006 baseball draft. He admits that he almost didn't go back to school because he was so disappointed, but he hung in there, he did go back to school—and he ended up being drafted in the 12th round of the 2007 draft. After the draft, Vogt told the *Los Angeles Times*, "One of the biggest things I learned from the coaching staff at Azusa Pacific is that baseball is a game of attrition. You've got to grind it out, and you have to earn everything in life."

Former MLB pitcher Jack Cassel spent 7 seasons in the minor leagues and was released during spring training. He then re-signed and went to AAA baseball, but was soon demoted. At that point, he admits, he considered retiring, but, instead, he worked on his game and strengthened his confidence through his improvement. In fact, his coach credits his difficult years as having ultimately helped him when he *finally did make it to the pros*.

Jim Abbott, former pro baseball pitcher and now a motivational speaker, likes to talk about his very own personal example of resilience (beyond the fact that he became a pitcher with only one hand). Specifically, Abbott had a week in which he threw a no-hitter—*right after pitching a game where he had surrendered 7 runs and 10 hits in 31/2 innings*. Says Abbott, "I was frustrated, down and disappointed. I was wondering how I was going to turn it around, and then five days later I had one of the great moments of my whole life [the no-hitter]. The point," he says, "is that you might be down now, but you don't know what's going to happen tomorrow."

It takes great resilience to recover almost immediately from a significant mistake during a competition, and figure skater Jeremy Abbott exhibited just that on the world stage during the 2014 Olympics. After a serious fall during his performance, he came back to his feet and performed the rest of the routine smoothly. Explaining his response to the fall, he told an interviewer, "The second I stood up and the crowd started screaming, I had to finish ... My personal story has always been about perseverance and always getting up when you fall; so maybe I'm not an Olympic Champion but, if nothing else, I can teach the world that."

Finally ... on a different note: Lorenza Munoz wrote an insightful essay that appeared in the *Los Angeles Times* about the fact that she did not persevere in swimming; and she wistfully describes her past abilities as an "Olympic-caliber" swimmer. She says she let "insignificant issues" keep her from achieving her once-possible Olympic goals, explaining that it was her nationality and her emotional response to the bureaucracy around it that "shut her down."

"This year, as I do every four years, I will watch the opening ceremonies at the Olympics and cry," wrote Munoz. "It won't be out of idealism or patriotism, but regret ... Swimming was the test of my young life and I failed because I was preoccupied with things that didn't matter. ... When I watch the world's best swimmers parade behind their flags this summer, I'll wish one more time that I had known then what I know so clearly now: Sports isn't about fairness, but mental toughness."

COMPETITIVE SPIRIT ..."HEART"

The "competitive streak" that is a part of the soul of every single successful athlete is a concept that doesn't get as much attention as do "natural talent" and "hard work." But, after researching the topic extensively, it is clear that the competitive spirit is at least as important as natural talent, and at least as important as hard work. Without it, the talent may survive, but the motivation to work hard will eventually fade. In other words, competitive spirit seems to be an equal part of the "success equation."

In interview after interview, athletes talk about the need to "get better than the other guys" — "work harder than the other guys" — "beat the other guys." (With individual sports, the "other guy" they are trying to beat is most likely to be "themselves" and their "personal best.") Successful athletes talk about the sense of competition as their motivation; they talk about it as their gratification; and they talk about it as their reason to strive to eventually play in the big leagues.

Considering the competitive spirit in a slightly different way, philosophy professor Andrew Bernstein talked about an athlete's "soul" in the *USA Today* series about "The Soul of a Champion." Dr. Bernstein explained that, "It's in someone's moral character—some indefatiguable quality that a person has that they're not going to be denied."

As Olympic soccer star Tiffeny Milbrett was quoted on the *JockBio.com* website: "Do you have the heart to push yourself? If you don't, find a way to get it because talent will only get you so far. You've got to be hungry. You've got to have heart. That's just reality."

You either have it or you don't. That's what some experts believe about the "competitive streak." Do you perceive that to be true, or not? In fact, when thinking about the importance of the significant competitive spirit that successful athletes must possess ... think about your own children. Think about yourself. Do you think a competitive spirit is "natural" or do you think it can be developed? Do you think a competitive spirit can be instilled in your child?

Just ask yourself these questions: *If you consider yourself to be a competitive person, do you think there is anything anyone can do to make you less competitive? If you are not a competitive person, do you think there is anything anyone can do to make you more competitive—to make you care more about whether you win or lose when competing? And, think about this: is your competitive spirit (or lack thereof) generally the same as it was when you were 5 or 10 or 15 years old?*

These are important questions to consider when guiding your children through their youth sports experiences. Your expectations have to be realistic, in terms of their drive, their desire, and their approach to competition. Without a significantly competitive nature, they will have limitations that you, and they, might not even currently recognize.

On the other hand, if you truly believe that a competitive streak can be instilled in a child, go ahead and try to find a way to instill it. See how it works; and good luck with that. But note in several of the following anecdotes that successful athletes often talk about memories of *always* having been competitive—even when they were young.

Said soccer star Mia Hamm in a *USA Today* interview: "When I was little, people always used to say, 'It doesn't matter if you win or lose.' Well, to me it did."

In a "Hershey's Presents Parents & Kids" article, baseball star Andy Pettitte's parents claimed that they saw his competitive spirit at a very young age, and they described how they remember him crying after a flag football game—at the age of 6—because his teammates weren't taking the game seriously.

Soccer star Landon Donovan began playing soccer at a very young age and reportedly "loved it" from the start. But noteworthy is that he has also been described as always having had "an intense, all-consuming desire to win" by those who knew him when he was young.

Former competitive swimmer and triathlete Hayley Peirsol claims that it was competing against her brothers that made her the star swimmer she became, because—as she said in an interview— "I was so competitive, especially with my brothers. I would never let them beat me."

Though the nature of competition is to ultimately "win" the competition, it is interesting to note that many athletes don't talk specifically about "winning" when they refer to their competitive drive. They, instead, talk about "hating to lose." Think about it. There is a distinct difference between the concept of "winning" and the concept of "not losing." In fact, based on the research, it seems that "hating to lose" perhaps has a little more power over many athletes than does "loving to win."

Famed sportswriter Dan Jenkins commented on this concept in a *HuffingtonPost.com* interview. Said Jenkins; "The thing I always thought, and I don't know if its true or not, but everybody wants to win and everyone says they want to win, but the great champions absolutely despised the idea of losing."

Softball star Jennie Finch has admitted, "I hate losing. I mean, I love winning, but losing is a much more intense feeling."

Olympic Gold medalist Michael Phelps once explained that he trained hard because he hated losing. "If I didn't swim my best I'd think about it at school, at dinner, with my friends. It would drive me crazy."

It might put a smile on your face to know that LeBron James actually admitted to *Sports Illustrated Kids* that he doesn't play one-on-one basketball because he's not very good at it ... and he "doesn't want to lose."

Former baseball pro Curt Schilling's comments from a *USA Today* article also provide insight into this discussion. Said

Schilling, "I hated losing. That was how I was wired, not how I was coached or parented."

Part of the motivation to "not lose" can be an athlete's "fear of failure," according to sports psychologists. (This, in particular, is a big topic in their practices.) It's a complicated topic, and one that will just be touched on here, but one thing is clear: the "fear of failure" can work against an athlete, or it can work for an athlete. It's all about the processing of the emotions.

The great football receiver Jerry Rice talked about his "fear of failure" in his Hall of Fame speech—admitting that he played football with that very fear. He said he "ran scared"; he ran "with a fear of getting caught"; and he says he could "hear and feel" the defender chasing him, making "the hairs on the back of his neck stand up."

Rice went on to point out that this fear of being caught is what made him work harder than anyone else, every single day. "I'm here to tell you," said Rice, "that the fear of failure is the engine that has driven me throughout my entire life. It flies in the faces of all these sports psychologists who say you have to let go of your fears to be successful and that negative thoughts will diminish performance. But not wanting to disappoint my parents, and later my coaches, teammates and fans, is what pushed me to be successful."

Many athletes also talk about their intense desire to "prove someone wrong" or to "prove to someone that they could do it." And sometimes they just have to prove it to themselves. This is particularly true with those who have always been "underestimated," as discussed in a previous chapter.

One example: As discussed in a *Jockbio.com* profile, Toronto's draft selection of future baseball star Vernon Wells was widely criticised in 1997 (Wells was 18), but Wells says he refused to let the criticism affect him negatively; instead, he was determined to use the critical comments as motivation and prove everyone wrong. So he clipped news articles and read stories on the Internet and he remembered them. He did, indeed, prove that Toronto did not make a mistake.

NFL star quarterback Aaron Rodgers (Associated Press Male Athlete of the Year in 2011 and Super Bowl MVP) obviously became extremely successful in the NFL, even though he was rejected by most college football programs coming out of high school. According to an article in *Sports Illustrated Kids*, Rodgers kept the rejection letters from college football programs, and he even leaves a few of them around his house to this day. Explains Rodgers, "I chose the couple that I thought were the most demeaning to display in a space in my house that really nobody is able to see but myself. It's something that I think is important to keep fresh on your mind. ... and you have a little laugh about the journey you've been on ... at the same time remembering that there still are people out there that you can prove something to."

In an article by the Positive Coaching Alliance titled "Lessons Learned from the 2010 Giants World Series Victory," the point was made that "the key ingredient in the team's victory was "effort"—the team was determined to overcome the perception that they were an underdog."

Said NFL running back Tim Hightower, when he was discussing the initial lack of interest in him by the NFL: "I'm a guy who is always trying to prove somebody wrong." With that spirit,

Hightower ended up setting a Cardinals rookie record for rushing touchdowns in a season—proving a lot of people wrong.

James Harrison, 2008 NFL Defensive Player of the Year and Super Bowl starter, was cut 4 different times by teams; but it only made him more competitive and more determined. As he told the *Baltimore Sun*, "People said I was too short, too slow, couldn't do this or that. I try not to look back, but I prepare myself every off-season with thoughts of what people said I couldn't do. Nobody believed I could play."

The NFL's Adam Vinatieri was quoted in *USA Today* as claiming that even though he had been to the Super Bowl 6 times in 11 years, he felt that he had to "re-prove" himself each time he stepped on the field.

Before the NBA draft, Derrick Williams told *Sporting News;* "Whoever does choose me is making the right choice and whoever doesn't choose me ... I will try to get back at them and let them know they should have chosen me." (He was drafted 2nd overall in the 2011 draft, by the Timberwolves.)

Even though he set his high school record for home runs, Ryan Howard (2005 NL Rookie of the Year and 2006 National League MVP) told *SIKids.com* that he was ignored by major league scouts and by most major colleges coming out of high school because they thought he wasn't a good enough all-around player. So his high school coach personally called the coach at Missouri State, and Howard was offered a chance to walk on. Quickly proving what a good baseball player he was, Howard claimed, "I liked having to prove myself. I wanted to see how good I really was."

Mike Pringle, a record-setting Hall of Fame running back in the Canadian Football League, admits that he went to the Canadian League out of frustration after being cut by the NFL after only 3 games. He also points out that his disappointing NFL experience motivated him to succeed in the CFL. Says Pringle, "I always had a chip on my shoulder. I was always trying to get back down to the NFL."

Finally ... Michael Jordan's competitive streak is legendary, and was described in a *Los Angeles Times* commentary this way by Bulls President John Paxson: "He [Jordan] didn't accept failure in anything. [But] he wasn't afraid to fail, because how many times did he put the game on his shoulders and win it? There was something unique about that mentality that I can't describe." And, as Jordan's former coach Doug Collins has said, "Michael competes in everything. He's driven by competition.

IS IT EFFORT?

HARD WORK!

No amount of talent will get an athlete far without the addition of extremely hard work. Successful athletes work extremely hard, regardless of whether they have "talent" or not—and regardless of their age. In fact, for some athletes, their actual "talent" may very well be their special ability to work very, very hard.

Researcher and psychologist Dr. Anders Ericsson explains in the book *Freakonomics*; "I think the most general claim here is that a lot of people believe there are some inherent limits they were born with. But there is surprisingly little hard evidence that anyone could attain any kind of exceptional performance without spending a lot of time perfecting it." He goes on to explain, "This is not to say that all people have equal potential. Michael Jordan, even if he hadn't spent countless hours in the gym, would still have been a better basketball player than most of us. But without those hours in the gym, he would never have become the player he was."

In an *ESPNW* interview, WNBA star Kaleena Mosqueda-Lewis said, "I don't think anyone has a limit. As hard as you're willing to work is as far as you're able to go."

If there is only one concept that both parents and kids take away from this book, I hope it is this one: that *NO ONE SUCCEEDS IN SPORTS WITHOUT REALLY, REALLY HARD WORK*—not Kobe Bryant, not LeBron James, not Tom Brady. It is so important that kids understand that, and it is likely that many really don't. How could they understand how hard their athlete heros work? They don't see signs of it anywhere. Successful athletes make the sport they play look so easy and fun; they make it look like they are always in control, like they always know what to do and where to be. And they always seem to be in great shape—naturally. No one on the outside sees the hours and hours of daily practice, the training of the mind and body; they see the fun and the games. And how could even most older high school kids really understand the concept thoroughly, when they feel like they are working hard, themselves, but not seeing enough success?

As demonstrated by real-world examples of hard work: there is hard work, and then there is ... HARD WORK! Successful athletes work harder than others because they are never satisfied, and they always feel that there is room for improvement.

As NFL defensive end Mario Williams told *SIKids.com*; "It feels good to be on a list of Top 5 Defensive Ends of the Decade, but at the same time, you try to go out and get better every day." He also insisted; "No matter how well I did on a pass rush, how hard I thought I hit someone, there's always a possibility to do it better. You have to think that way! There's no way you can improve otherwise."

First round draft pick Lucas Giolito, with his 100 mph fastball, still feels the need to continue working hard. As he told *Calihighsports.com*, "I've always worked hard. Whether it's in the weight room or on the field. Also, I've lived with my personal goal and saying 'something can always be better.' "

When I, myself, have discussed the issue of "hard work" in sports with many former "less-than-successful" athletes, some have scoffed at the idea that successful athletes really do work very hard—calling it a "cliche," or arguing that "all athletes say that because it sounds good." Similar to Geoff Colvin's theory about why people resist the notion that "talent is overrated," could it be that these cynics don't want to believe that hard work might be the primary component to success in sports ... perhaps because that would mean that they could have been more successful if they had worked harder?

One of the key early experiences I had that influenced me to develop this book was talking to former Indiana University basketball coach Mike Davis on a plane many years ago—the year after he took on the Indiana program and replaced the infamous Bobby Knight. At the time, Indiana was considered one of the best basketball schools to play for, so Coach Davis had the "pick of the litter" when recruiting. And since he actually happened to be on a recruiting trip at the time, I quizzed him about what he looked for in order to make recruiting decisions.

Davis explained that all of the recruits he would talk to would be equally capable: they all could play basketball well enough to play at a Division I level. So he said that he was more interested in understanding their "work ethic"—looking for clues to their attitude and willingness to work hard. He also emphasized that there would be many very good high school basketball players who would never go much further in basketball, simply because they wouldn't be willing to work hard enough in a college program.

Hard work is hard. And it is work. It's not fun, as we all well know. And even when working hard at a sport, it's not fun. It's work. An athlete, regardless of the age or skill level, has to have motivation to put the hours into hard work at his/her sport, and the hard work has to be directed at not only the fun aspects of the sport, but the not-so-fun areas, as well—which is a particularly difficult thing for young athletes to do. (It can be equally difficult for many older athletes, too.)

Sports psychologist Dr. Bob Rotella talks about this very topic in his book *The Golfer's Mind*, pointing out that "the biggest difference between professional and amateur golfers is their "skill with the scoring clubs"—the high number clubs, wedges and putter." Most amateur golfers aren't practicing with these important clubs around the green because they would rather be at the driving range. It's more fun!

A *Sports Illustrated* article by Lee Jenkins told a story about LeBron James and his continuous hard work. Jenkins described how James struggled emotionally after the Heat's loss to the Mavericks in the 2011 NBA championship, so LeBron went back to Ohio to train with his former coach at his high school, Keith Dambrot. Said Dambrot, "He [LeBron] wants the truth. He's not too big to take criticism. I told him, 'You have to do more things you don't want to do ... all the basics that made you great going back to the beginning.' " LeBron proceeded to work on his game intensely, according to Dambrot. Commented Miami coach Erik Spoelstra, after that period: "The great always stay uncomfortable. LeBron is no different. He came back looking like a new player."

Former NFL star Clay Matthews, Jr. talks about the same type of hard work when he now coaches young athletes. He tells them, "Take pride in the things you don't want to do. In football, out of 10 things that you've got to do [in practice], 8 of them are probably unpleasant. You have to learn to take pride in those 8, and then enjoy the other 2."

Regarding the previously discussed problem of "early bloomers" who often don't develop a work ethic, Dr. Malcolm Conway (*Raising Elite Athletes*) explains that many kids who seem to "just have it" and seem to be able to do it all at a young age sometimes end up resting on their laurels. As a result, their "talent levels" slowly erode because they have not learned the discipline of the hard work they need to do in order to take their abilities to the next level. Conway also writes that he has sometimes seen young, "less-than-average" players work their way up to Division I scholarships because they understood that—through endless hard work—they could develop the skills needed for that level of play.

Throughout my research I found no better example of the real-world hard work that is required to not only succeed in a sport, but to stay successful in a sport, than a description of the work ethic of the great Kobe Bryant. Wouldn't you think that, by now, Kobe could sort of relax a little bit, rest on his laurels a little bit, and maintain his skills just by playing the game? A lot of kids and adults probably assume that is exactly what he does. But, according to *Businessinsider.com* writer Tony Manfred, Kobe *still* has super intense workouts on game days; *still* trains for 4 hours a day during the season (and more than that off-season); *still* tries out new moves on other players after practice; *still* counts all of his made shots in practice, and only stops when he gets to 400; *still* plays one-on-one games to 100.......

Explaining his work ethic, Kobe, himself, says he wants to be remembered "as a person that's over-achieved; that would mean a lot to me. That means I put a lot of work in and squeezed every ounce of juice out of this orange that I could."

There are three NFL players in the Gronkowski family (1 in 31 millions odds, according to *ESPN.com*). And though anyone might assume that genetics play a large role in this family, their father has emphasized the role that hard work plays in the boys' athletic success. He points out in an *ESPN.com* interview that, "I don't think any of them went three days without working out—since eighth grade."

Professional golfer Jason Day has said that he practiced golf 32 hours a week as a teen at his boarding school, and that all he did was go to school and play golf. After high school he quickly and impressively did well enough on the Nationwide Tour to make it to the next and highest level, the PGA Tour. But Day admitted in a *USA Today* interview that, after he excelled early on in the Nationwide Tour, "I thought I was going to get a PGA Tour win a lot quicker than I did. I took it for granted and didn't work hard enough. I thought it would come easy and it doesn't come easy. I learned again it takes a lot of hard work and dedication."

Hall of Famer Jerry Rice also expressed an understanding of that concept when he told *ESPN* that, even though he was considered one of the best receivers of all time, "No one was going to work harder than me, and if I didn't, the kid coming out of college would take my job."

Talking about how hard Tom Brady works, former college quarterback and current quarterback coach Scott Loeffler once said in *Sports Illustrated*, "He [Brady] is 34 years old [at the time] and approaches the game like he just got drafted in the sixth round." (Recall that he *did* get drafted in the 6th round—and that keeps him motivated.)

As Olympic gold medalist Dana Vollmer explained in a *Good Morning America* interview, an athlete has to keep pushing. "Anyone can perform well when they feel great, but what defines an athlete is what they do when they don't feel great. Think about that as you're training and pushing yourself. It does hurt sometimes and that's what makes it worth it."

Baseball great Josh Hamilton may, indeed, have "natural talent." But, more importantly, he reportedly loved playing baseball so much as a teenager that he made it his primary activity. In fact, sports writer Tim Stevens covered Hamilton locally when he was in high school and once wrote; "Josh Hamilton said his summer job between his junior and senior year in high school was baseball." And when Stevens asked Hamilton what he did after a baseball game or practice, Hamilton replied, "I come home and I hit." Stevens further wrote, "He [Hamilton] was all baseball. That was his life." (*from SportsIllustrated.com*)

Soccer superstar Mia Hamm told *USA Today*; "Some people think they can train two or three times a week instead of seven or eight. They think they can take a day off. The great ones don't."

NFL Hall of Fame member Curtis Martin credits his work ethic for his long career, and explained to the *New York Post*; "Much of it [success] was just pure determination. I still maintained the belief that every year there was someone on the team who was more gifted than I was ... I don't know if they necessarily had more talent as a package, but I feel like they had more ability. I just focused on outworking everyone."

Even at a fairly young age, some relatively successful athletes recognize the importance of really hard work, and they are willing to do it. For example, in an *ESPN.com* article discussing Damon Harge—who was ranked the top 6th grade basketball player in the nation in 2012—his coach was quoted as saying; "Damon's work ethic is what makes him stand out. The 12-year old wakes up at 4:30 every morning and puts in an average of 6,500 shots per week. With that high volume of shots the muscle memory is ridiculous."

High school wide receiver Trenton Irwin, the first freshman to start on the varsity football team at his California high school, is described as such a dedicated hard worker that he "catches up to 1,500 balls a lot of weekends."

And said the coach of Jahlil Okafor, a Chicago high school basketball player who is the top player in the class of 2014, "He's [Okafor] so hungry to get better. Last summer he was playing on the junior USA team in Mexico, and the night he got back to Chicago he called me up to make sure he could get in the gym the next afternoon."

The high school coach of Curtis Beach, a decathlete who set a national record in 2009, said of his star: "Curtis's motivation, desire, and work ethic supersede his great talent. He will work endlessly. Lots of people see the talent. I see the endless, endless work."

In a *Los Angeles Times* article about professional baseball player Chase Utley, his former coach, Joe Perruccio, reportedly said that Utley "didn't have a lot of natural ability. But he did the hard work. He just loved playing the game. And, then, when he was relegated to being only a designated hitter his first year at UCLA, he worked harder on defense to get his glove back."

Michael Phelps has been quoted as saying that he credits much of his success to training: "I knew nobody was going to work harder than me." He also spoke of his 7-day-a-week training regimen in a talk I heard him give, and he insisted that he never took Sundays off in practice—because he knew all the other swimmers he was competing against did.

In a Charlie Rose interview of author Geoff Colvin (*Talent is Overrated*), Colvin tells of someone asking tennis great Martina Navratilova, *How many hours do I have to practice to be a champion?* and Navratilova answered, "If you have to ask that question, you will never be a champion."

Ian Thomsen wrote an article about the 2011 NBA draft on *SportsIllustrated.com* which was entitled, "NBA Draft Long on Overachievers." In it he wrote, "This NBA draft may have been short on All-Star talent, but it could be strong in leadership. Many of the lottery picks earned their way to high first-round salaries because they were able to overcome deficiencies in athleticism or size—which says a lot for their character as basketball players."

Thomsen went on to point out that "an admirable work ethic was one of the often overlooked intangibles that was abundant in this draft" and that "there weren't a lot of blue-ribbon stars to choose from, but there were many blue-collar workers."

WORK ETHIC: It is impossible to discuss the role of "hard work" without mentioning the extreme importance of having a "work ethic" in order to succeed at sports. Though it is difficult to define "work ethic," it generally implies that an athlete is dedicated, positive and determined to work hard and practice his/her sport in the proper way. And he/she does it with a great attitude and a consistency of never letting up. In fact, this aspect of development is so important that most coaches mention it when they talk about the superior facets of a successful athlete. It goes hand-in-hand with the concept of hard work, in general.

Important to note: Child development experts will say, over and over again, that the *motivation* to work exceptionally hard at a sport can't be forced by anyone on the outside. It can't come from coaches and it can't come from parents. It has to come from within. Of course coaches can force hard work upon their players, with demands of drills and workouts, but true motivation is different than that; it is an intangible force that goes beyond the drills and the workouts. As former NFL General Manager Scott Pioli said, "You can teach someone work habits—you can't teach work ethic." (From a talk at the MIT Sports Analytics Conference)

Perhaps it is time for American kids to develop a better work ethic. According to San Antonio Spurs Coach Gregg Popovich, "Foreign players are fundamentally harder working than most American kids," and that is why more than half of his team consists of players from outside the United States—according to an *ESPN The Magazine* article. The story, written by Seth Wickersham, goes on to explain that Popovich feels that American athletes "have been coddled since eighth, ninth, tenth grade by various factions or groups of people. But the foreign kids don't live with that. So they don't feel entitled."

Finally ... one of the most profound comments I uncovered about the concept of hard work (in any endeavor) was stated by the very wise and successful author Malcolm Gladwell, who wrote; "It's really risky to work hard, because then if you fail you can no longer say that you failed because you didn't work hard. It's a form of self-protection."

PRACTICE APPROACH/STYLE

"It's true," neuroscientists say. "Practice does make perfect!" There are different concepts of "practice," however, so it is worthwhile for kids to learn the differences when they are young. Young athletes often mistakenly believe that "putting the time in" is the same thing as hard work, and they often think that "being at practice" for their sport is equivalent to practicing their sport. But practice is not that simple, and practice style can vary from athlete to athlete and sport to sport.

Of course, in youth sports, much of any organized practice is controlled by coaches, and athletes have to do what is expected of them. The real work, however, can take place outside of formal practices ... and that's what successful athletes do. They don't wait for someone to tell them to practice in their free time, and they don't rely on others to motivate them to practice. They practice on their own, because they enjoy the process of working towards getting better.

While this section is not intended to specifically instruct any coaches or athletes regarding practice style, the following briefly introduces concepts that can be explored further by anyone involved with the development of young athletes, including parents. Kids can also get something from these ideas.

There are new ideas about practice approach being presented by researchers, trainers, and coaches frequently, with one of the more recent and widely discussed being the "10,000–Hour Rule." Described by author Malcolm Gladwell in his book *Outliers*, this "rule" suggests that it takes about *10,000 hours* of dedicated practice to truly master a skill. A variation of the 10,000-Hour Rule is the "10 Year Rule," as described by author Geoff Colvin in his book, *Talent is Overrated*. That concept claims that it takes at least *10 years* of hard work to achieve excellence at any sport.

Obviously, these concepts are based on time spent in practice, but they are not quite that simple. There is much more to them than simply spending the time in practice, and the books provide more detail.

In addition to the time spent in practice, the *quality* of practice is a key issue among experts. An article written by athletic trainer Judd Biasiotto on *StrengthPlanet.com* talks about the substance of world class/elite athletes, and makes a very clear point: "According to sports researcher John Lather, the #1 variable related to elite performance is time spent in training ... . But Lather also emphasizes that it is *quality training* that is required—not just *time*. Says Lather; "Most successful athletes train in a wide variety of ways, but they all train with high intensity and purpose." In fact, it is a common principle among most sports trainers and coaches that the level of intensity during practice has to be the same as if in a game, and that lowering standards for practice will have a negative effect on ultimate performance.

Researcher Dr. Anders Ericsson has looked extensively at learning and memory through his research on performance. As a result, he has come to refer to a specialized process of practice as "deliberate practice"— as explained in the book *Freakonomics*. Also, Geoff Colvin delves into the contemporary body of scientific research regarding sports performance and the brain in his book, *Talent is Overrated*: he discusses the concept of "deliberate practice," as well.

Just briefly, the fundamentals of "deliberate practice" are that a person sets specific goals for himself/herself while practicing, obtains immediate feedback, and then concentrates on technique along with outcome—as opposed to simply repeating a task over and over again the same way. (There is more specific information about these ideas in the books mentioned.)

Along similar lines, an article on the website *Responsiblesports.com* reports that kids learn faster from mistakes than from repetitive "correct" practice—even though the conventional wisdom in sports is that kids learn best when they practice the "right" way to do something over and over. More than one study is cited in the article that supports this concept, but the writer specifically refers to a psychological study that points out that "athletes who have a 'growth' mindset are more successful than those athletes with a 'fixed' mindset." (A growth mindset loves a challenge and learns by making mistakes, while a "fixed" mindset relies on innate talents, and fears failure.)

Following are real-world athletes' experiences with their own practice styles:

As a senior in high school, runner Alan Webb was the first to run a sub-4-minute high school indoor mile, even though he didn't switch from swimming to running until his freshman year. Webb credited his rapid success to the fact that "other high schoolers seemed to fear the necessary speedwork ... they were too comfortable training at a slower pace and sought sanctuary in slow-paced training." But Webb focused more on speed than they did, working toward that race for 2 years and training with speedwork. He has said that he was also a "student of running"—reading everything he could about the sport.

The high school coach of NBA star Jeremy Lin blamed Lin's practice approach in high school for his *delayed* success, and he also gave credit to Lin's later practice approach for his *ultimate* success. As the coach told *ESPN*, "Jeremy was not a good practice player [in high school]." But after a year playing basketball at Harvard, Lin went back to his high school coach and asked him to help him work out. Said the coach; "From that point on, a workout fiend was born. During the lockout, Lin's schedule read like a brochure for Navy SEAL BUD/S training."

The father of Major League Baseball's Daniel Nava has described how he helped his son compensate for his small size by developing his hitting skills—making him a skilled switch hitter by never allowing him to bat left or right twice in a row.

Many successful athletes perfected their athletic skills simply by playing games in the neighborhood as kids. For example, pro baseball pitcher Dontrelle Willis told *Sports Illustrated Kids* that he developed his "big leg kick" as a kid by playing a game with friends that they called "strikeout." "We always used to do different things to create deception, and my delivery just kind of evolved into the way it is now," said Willis.

Freddy Adu, a soccer phenom at the age of 13, told *60 Minutes* that the reason he got so good so fast was that, "I did not go one day without playing. I was just kicking and learning. It was awesome, because, you know, like there was no coaches, no one to tell you what to do. It was just, you play and learn stuff on your own."

Left-handed hitter Todd Helton became one of baseball's top all-around batters through mastering the art of hitting to the opposite field. He explained in *Sports Illustrated Kids* that, even though he was always a lefty, he had to practice hitting balls to the left instead of the natural direction to the right when he was a kid— because he practiced hitting into a net in his basement, and the family's boat was on the right side of the basement.

NBA Rookie of the Year, Tyreke Evans, grew up in a rough neighborhood and had three older brothers who basically raised him and protected him. According to a *New York Times* article, one brother started coaching him in basketball from the age of four; one brother helped him develop moves and dribbling skills; and one brother worked with him on shooting skills—making him take 1200-1500 shots every other day.

Mahmoud Abdul-Rauf became one of basketball's best free throw shooters through his compulsive need to practice shooting free throws until he was able to hit 10 free throws in a row. (He has Tourette's Syndrome, which caused the clinically compulsive behavior.)

NFL quarterback Dan Orlovsky told *YourCT.com*; "When I was younger I would have garbage cans set up all around the yard and I would have, like, 20 balls and just fire them into the cans. I really had nothing else to do back then."

And when recent NFL draftee Brandon Williams had a job working with portable toilets, he "pretended the outhouses were offensive linemen when he was lifting them into his truck. I acted like I was playing football. I just made it fun," said Williams.

Finally ... according to *ThePostGame.com*, Oregon State football might have started a team practice trend with their use of a DJ and music during practices. When coach Mike Riley first had the music played during practice, the players immediately responded to it. "At first I started dancing, and then I was shocked," running back Storm Woods told USA Today. "It made practice more fun, more intense. Guys were flying around. It was a different atmosphere. A better one."

According to the article, Texas A&M and Louisiana-Lafayette have jumped on board with the same idea, and ... the Super Bowl winning Seattle Seahawks reportedly incorporated music into their practice routines last season! (By the time you're reading this, no doubt many other teams will have started practicing with music, as well.)

IS IT ATTITUDE?

WILLINGNESS TO SACRIFICE

Though the sacrifices experienced by young athletes were noted in an earlier chapter, the willingness to make significant personal sacrifices must continue more intensely as athletes progress.

As the father of Lucas Giolito (a first-round MLB pick in 2012) explained in a *calihighsports.com* interview; "I tried to explain to him [Lucas] that he would have to learn to make some sacrifices that other kids may not be asked to do in terms of freedom he might expect as a kid. This included missing social events because he had made a commitment to the game and teams he was playing on. He took it very seriously. Only twice since he was 11 years old has he asked to miss a practice to go to a birthday party or just hang out with a friend."

Olympic medalist snowboarder Gretchen Bleiler's mother told *NBC News* that Gretchen "put in the hours and worked and did what it took ... If that meant being on the hill when all her friends were at the movies, that's what she did."

The high school best friend of pro basketball player Dwight Howard said in a *USA Today* article about Howard; "His work ethic was such that he stayed in the gym. When the rest of us would go off to the movies, he would be in the gym."

Jackie Elliott, the Montana Gatorade Soccer Player of the Year in 2010-2011, was offered both a basketball scholarship and a soccer scholarship out of high school (she also had a 4.0 GPA).

As she explained in an interview on *Gatorade.com*, "It takes a lot of sacrifice. Sometimes you just have to stay home and study or practice instead of going out and having fun."

HUMILITY

It would be naive to claim that most successful athletes are truly humble. But it would be safe to say that most of the truly successful and—more importantly—well-respected athletes do express themselves with humility. They treat their teammates, coaches, and opponents with an attitude of humility, and they evaluate their own skills with a degree of humility. Most importantly, it is difficult to improve skills without the ability to recognize, and admit, that there is room for skill improvement—and that someone else might be able to contribute to that skill improvement.

Humility is probably a difficult concept for kids to understand, but it doesn't have to be a difficult concept to teach to kids. Here is Daniel Webster's definition of "humility," for guidance: *"Absence of pride or self-assertion."* But now considering that definition, it only makes the issue more confusing. Shouldn't kids take "pride" in what they do? Shouldn't they "assert" themselves in sports activities? Of course. But humility is represented by the manner in which pride and assertion are exhibited.

Social psychologist Wade Rowatt discussed humility in athletes in an article in *Psychology Today* in this way: "Humility leads to an understanding that 'I'm not always the best, and that another person on any given day can win.' If you look at the best athletes," says Rowatt, "most display this sort of respect for opponents."

It goes without saying that kids who brag and are "less than humble" get knocked down by their peers and teammates quite often, and they can even lose playing time and/or support because of their attitude. But a lack of humility can continue into college and the pros, where the athlete can get knocked down even harder—by teammates, coaches, the press, and the public. There are many examples in sports where a lack of humility hurt an athlete's draft potential, their team standing, their image, etc...

Most recently, the Seattle Seahawks' Richard Sherman created a firestorm when he "ranted" after making a game-winning play. His behavior brought up the subject of humility in the press and among fans, and was hotly debated as to whether it was appropriate or not. The incident did affect his image, at least in the short-run.

Sherman's rant wasn't the first or the worst, and it won't be the last. In fact, the "historical" poster child for lack of humility in professional sports could arguably be baseball Hall of Famer Rickey Henderson, who reportedly had a public image of arrogance—particularly because of the way he expressed himself. Most notably, in the speech he gave after breaking Lou Brock's stolen base record, he referred to himself as "the greatest of all-time"—a description that brought immediate negative reaction from the press and public. (Even though he was the "greatest of all-time" at stealing bases.)

In a later interview with *Baseball Digest*, Henderson discussed the comment, saying, "As soon as I said it, it ruined everything. Everyone thought it was the worst thing you could ever say. Those words haunt me to this day and will continue to haunt me. They over-shadow what I've accomplished in this game."

After his playing career had ended, Henderson was still sensitive to the impact of his comments; but he perhaps made up for them in his Hall of Fame speech when he said, "And now that the association has voted me into the Baseball Hall of Fame, my journey as a player is complete. I am now in a class of the greatest players of all time and at this moment, I am .... very, very humbled."

In another example of both humility and lack, thereof, an article on *NCAA.com* describes college golfer Scott Strohmeyer as "a stubborn son of a gun when he arrived at Alabama as a freshman in 2008." Admitted Strohmeyer, himself; "I thought I knew everything. I thought I knew how to play golf. I was like, 'Who's this coach trying to tell me how to play golf?' " But fortunately for Strohmeyer, he says he eventually "humbled myself and let Coach coach me."

Though it didn't happen overnight, Strohmeyer and his coach, Jay Seawell, eventually connected, and the Alabama golf team captured the Division I Men's Golf Championship during Strohmeyer's senior year. Strohmeyer was team captain.

In an example of true humility, Major League Baseball player Tsuyoshi Nishioka made the following public comment after being released at the end of his second season by the Minnesota Twins. (He was reportedly released at his own request.) "I take full responsibility for my performance which was below my own expectations. At this time, I have made the decision that it is time to part ways. I have no regrets and know that only through struggle can a person grow stronger." To top it off, *Nishioka waved his right to his $3 million salary for the third year of his contract!*

Finally ... there is an old sports concept/saying that seems to define humility perfectly: *When you have success........... act like you have done it before*.

TEAMWORK

There are so many ways to teach the concept of teamwork to kids, and this responsibility generally falls on the shoulders of the coaches for any given sport. But parents have many opportunities to reinforce the concept. For example, a very important part of teamwork is the way a child responds to a coach, and this is where the parent can have an impact.

To give a little insight into the elements of teamwork, *Sports Illustrated Kids* published an article providing suggestions for how a child can be a good team member. It suggests that kids ...

... show respect to the coach.

... listen to the coach and wait until the coach is finished talking before speaking up at practice or during a game.

... ask questions. If you're not clear about something, ask the coach to explain it again.

... go all out. Show the coach that you want to improve by trying hard and staying focused at practice.

... let the coach talk to the refs---don't argue with the refs yourself.

(cont.)

... show sportsmanship. Keep your head in the game and cheer for your teammates—even if you're sitting on the bench.

... win with humility, lose with dignity. Don't show off when you win and don't sulk when you lose.

Jabari Parker was only the 4th high school non-senior to win the Gatorade National Player of the Year award in 2011, and was called "the best high school player since LeBron James," according to an article in *Sports Illustrated*. Related to this discussion on teamwork is the description of Parker's skills, provided by basketball talent evaluator Daniel Poneman: "He's [Parker] figured out how to dominate a game without scoring. He doesn't care if he scores 0 points or 50 as long as his team wins."

In a *USA Today* article, Arizona basketball coach Lute Olson pointed out that one of the many reasons he began recruiting Chase Budinger at 13 years old was because of his "unselfishness at such a young age." (Budinger does admit that coaches sometimes now tell him he passes too much.)

John Wooden was always a tremendous advocate for the importance of teamwork among his players, and he often said that two of the greatest players he coached were completely unselfish and team-oriented: Lew Alcindor (Kareem Abdul Jabbar) and Bill Walton. Explained Wooden, "They liked to score, but that was never first in their mind. It was always "we."

NFL safety Troy Palamalu has expressed his feelings about teamwork as, "The greatest joy I get is setting up plays for somebody else. I take a lot of pride in helping other people make plays."

LEADERSHIP

Of course not all successful athletes can be described as "leaders," but there are a few on every team that stand out from the crowd as true inspirational forces for their teammates. This holds true for even young athletic teams.

As sports psychologist Patrick Devine said in *Psychology Today*, "One of the most important things a leader does is promote the idea of task cohesion. He's the guy who can rally a team to work for a common goal instead of individual goals."

A few examples of leadership:

When referring to Stanford basketball player Jennifer Azzi after the team won its first national championship, Stanford player Angela Taylor was quoted as saying, "Jen was our best player and our hardest worker. Letting her down was worse than letting yourself down."

In a *Sports Illustrated* article, former Viking coach Bud Grant told how long-time team captain Jim Marshall was worshipped by both the fans and his teammates, and described him as "... a special kind of person. He was exactly what a captain should be. If I would say 'OK guys, let's do this,' Jim would be the first in line." If we had a rookie in the line-up he would say 'There goes Jim Marshall doing this full speed, full bore ... hey, I gotta do it." Added Grant, "Those are the kind of people you gotta have on a football team."

Referring to the leadership of former teammate Drew Brees, Jonathan Goodwin said, "When the best guy on the team is also the hardest worker, it's easy for guys to follow and believe in everything he says."

One of water polo's greatest players and coaches, Terry Schroeder—a four-time Olympian, the Olympic water polo team coach, and also a college coach—has always been known for his composure and leadership. About his former role as team captain, he has said, "I learned that the best kind of leadership comes from the *quiet man;* the one who leads by example. I always tried to be the first one in the water for practice; to work harder than anyone else."

Finally ... an example of how a lack of this quality can interfere with an otherwise high potential career. This story involves Geno Smith, a *second* round NFL draft pick in 2013 who supposedly expected to be drafted in the *first* round. He was extremely frustrated and disappointed by his second-round status, publicly blaming his agents, and firing them. But, according to some, the reason he dropped to the second round of the draft was actually because of his poor attitude and lack of leadership skills. As one league executive told *Yahoo!Sports*, "He [Smith] doesn't have much presence, not much of a leader. I don't think he's a bad person, but that's not enough to be a quarterback in this league." Then referring to E.J. Manuel, a draftee chosen ahead of Smith, another executive was quoted as saying, "Manuel gets it, he gets the whole big picture of what it takes to lead a team."

SUCCESSFUL SPORTS FAMILIES

Just as it is common for doctors to come from a family of doctors, teachers to come from a family of teachers, etc ... it is not uncommon for successful athletes to come from a family of athletes. However, while there is a perception among some that members of athletic families are successful in sports *primarily* because of genetics, there is much research to dispell that perception. Just as there is no "doctor gene" or "teacher gene"— there is probably no "athlete gene." There are a variety of dynamics in sports families that influence the future sports potential of its members.

Of course no one will argue against the suggestion that genetics do have some role, because they do, of course— particularly when it comes to body size and strength. And genetics probably play a larger role in some sports families than in others. WNBA player Cheryl Ford, the daughter of former NBA star Karl Malone, gives genes much of the credit for her success. As she told *Sports Illustrated Kids*; "People tell me all the time how much I am like my dad on the court. If I had a penny for every time people have said that, I'd be a millionaire. I am like him in everything. My height, my body, the way I move, everything."

Nevertheless, as with the influence of "natural talent" on athletic success, it is also a disservice to athletes who come from sports families to attribute their success primarily to genetics.

There is so much more that goes into the development of a successful athlete than just genetics. Athletic success was not promised to them at birth.

One interesting sports family example is that of Kobe Bryant and his father, Joe Bryant. Though Joe Bryant did play professional basketball outside of the United States and has coached extensively, *Sports Illustrated* writer Chris Ballard once wrote; "There is a common misconception that Kobe Bryant is just a younger, better version of his father—a chip off the old block." Ballard went on to explain that this perception is not correct, writing that the Lakers' Jerry West described the Bryants as "two entirely different people." He also wrote that Joe Bryant's former teammate, Steve Mix, has even said, "If you'd told me that of all the guys I played with, it was Joe Bryant who would produce one of the greatest players of the next generation, I never would have believed you." According to writer Ballard, "Joe never had the work ethic that Kobe has, or the determination."

So what exactly is the magic behind multiple generations of successful athletes in one family, if it is not primarily having genetically gifted physical talents? Is it a particular mindset that expects the continued sports legacy? Is it the exposure to professional sports that makes a child realize that playing at that level can be a reality, not just a fantasy? Is it the admiration (or rivalry) a younger sibling has for an older sibling? Is it the the need a child has to impress a parent? Is it the ability of a skilled parent to personally teach sports skills to their own child? Perhaps it is just having constant competition available. The answers: Research shows that it can be any number of these reasons.

An entire book could be written about just this topic alone, so this chapter will simply touch the surface of it and provide food for thought—and real-world insight as it relates to young athletic development.

Though admitting that they do have "great genes," college football player Jackson Jeffcoat and his college basketball playing twin sister, Jaqueline Jeffcoat, insist that their success is not necessarily due to only genes. (Their father was NFL defensive lineman Jim Jeffcoat.) As they told *USA Today*, "We've done a lot of hard work. We've been very motivated. That's how our family is—we like to compete." Jaqueline also added that their father "taught us so much about when we get to college what not to do and how to be coachable players. It would be a lot harder if he wasn't there. We've been prepared for things better than other kids."

Sportswriter Eric Sondheimer wondered, himself, about the influence that former baseball star Steve Garvey has had on his accomplished baseball-playing son, Ryan. He wrote, "Anyone who meets Ryan Garvey can sense the excitement and enthusiasm he has for baseball. Maybe it comes from meeting Hall of Famers. Maybe it comes from watching old videos of his father. Maybe it comes from hanging out with Lasorda, the always energetic former Dodgers manager who directed Steve Garvey to a world championship in 1981."

Throughout my research, the one feature of sports families that kept popping up was that the kids in these families grow up surrounded by a competitive environment, and they compete with each other from an early age. In other words, not only are they encouraged to be competitive, but they have a ready source of athletic, competitive foes. (Is there a competitive gene?)

A prime example of this is the Gronkowski family, with three of the five boys in the family playing in the NFL at the same time (Rob, Chris and Dan). According to an *ESPN.com* article, they were all genetically "big boys," and their father had college football experience; but their father also took their skill development into his own hands and specifically taught them "to be tough." As the elder Gronkowski told Eric Adelson of *ESPN.com*, "Robby and Chris ... the battles they used to have. Robby loved pain. They used to beat on the kid and he would come back for more."

Professional golfer Danielle Kang told *FORE* magazine that she took up golf in her early teen years because she got tired of hearing everyone talk about how great her older brother was at it. Explained Kang, "I was a bratty little child who needed all the attention. One day I said to my dad, 'Give me a club. I've got this.' "

Describing the influence of a competitive environment in more detail, Amy Wambach—professional soccer star/Olympic gold medalist/FIFA Player of the Year—told Martin Rogers of *Yahoo!Sports.com*; "My brothers were all athletes and I just grew up in an athletic family. There was always something going on with us. We were either playing lacrosse or hockey or basketball or rollerblading. Growing up as the youngest of seven was like being in a team environment; you learn all kinds of things. I learned how to compete, my brothers and sisters always played with me on the same level, and they never let me win until I was better than them and deserved it. Being in such a big family makes you humble. You might have a certain skill or talent, but there is always someone who is better at something than you."

There are the Cassel brothers (Matt, Jack and Justin), who play/played professional football and baseball. As Matt Cassel told the *Los Angeles Times*, "We like to push each other, but its not like a sibling rivalry or anything like that." And said their mom, "Every time they're together they have to have a flex-off. They have to see who has the biggest pecs. If anyone even started to look like they were out of shape, the other two were all over him." Also well-worth pointing out is a point made by *ESPN* that, "If Justin has learned anything from his older brothers, it's patience." (Note that the Cassel parents were not particularly successful athletes, themselves.)

Billy Donovan, University of Florida head basketball coach, had three players on his team at one time who were sons of professional athletes: Joakin Noah (father was a tennis pro), Al Horford (father was an NBA player), and Taurean Green (father was in the NBA). In a 2006 *Washington Post* interview, Coach Donovan had this to say about those three particular players and how they might have been influenced by their fathers' sports success: "They've never felt a sense of entitlement because their dads did this. I think Yannick Noah [Joakim's father] lining up and playing tennis against some of the great tennis players, he probably realized, "You know what? The guy across the net has as much talent as I do and what is it going to be that separates me from him? I'm sure when Sidney Green [Taurean's father] was lining up against some of the great power forwards of the NBA, he probably said, "You know what? This guy is as good as I am. What am I going to do?' I think that's helped those kids understand that the talent piece of it is a part of it, but the mental preparation and how hard you play and your team and winning is what it's all about."

Former NBA great Reggie Miller and his older sister, WNBA superstar Cheryl Miller, competed with each other on the basketball court from an early age. Cheryl was so skilled that she was the first woman on a basketball court to dunk: and Reggie's unusual, but very effective, shooting style was attributed to his learning to play ball against his skilled sister.

There are twins named Joe Rosa and Jim Rosa who are both quite accomplished middle-distance runners. They attribute their accomplishments to the fact that, from an early age, they competed against each other in everything they did. Not only did they push each other to run — and to run faster — but they tested each other in other ways, as well; for example ... *who could hold their breath under water the longest?*

College and World Cup soccer star Samantha Mewis's older sister, Kristie, played soccer in college, so Samantha had her to look up to, and to compete against while growing up. Said Samantha in a *USA Today* interview, "I've definitely learned a lot from her [Kristie]. She works really hard and I've seen all her successes because she works so hard and is so dedicated. I've taken a lot from that." Samantha also indicated that she and her sister were very competitive growing up and that Kristie "never took it easy on her." Said Samantha, "We compete against each other with just about everything, but it's good for us because we're only making each other better."

Similar to Samantha Mewis, UCLA soccer teammate Caprice Dydasco also developed her soccer game by playing against an older sibling — her brother, a high school Soccer Player of the Year. As the *Hawaii News Now* wrote, "Her [Caprice's] game blossomed thanks to backyard bouts with her brother Zane." Said Caprice, "I guess that really helped me as a player. I always got frustrated, but now I think when I play against my own age I'm confident because if I can take my brother, I can take someone my own age."

It has been said that, in the Manning family, Eli was not initially as interested in football as his big brothers Peyton and Cooper, but he learned the game because Peyton encouraged him to. (Cooper was also a very good football player.) Also, the three Manning boys were exposed to professional football through their father, former NFL star Archie Manning.

And then there are the Weaver brothers of Major League Baseball. Jered Weaver and Jeff Weaver grew up 6 years apart and, according to them, were not close at all because of the age difference. Since the Weaver brothers never even played baseball together, it is hard to say how they both ended up as MLB players, and even their father claims to be clueless. It apparently wasn't pressure from their parents, as their father has said that his main goal for them was to go to college and get an education—not to become major league baseball players. Some assume it was simply a strong case of looking up to an older brother and following in his footsteps.

Former professional tennis superstar Ivan Lendl had three US Open wins, three French Open wins, and three Australian Open wins, but he claims he didn't pressure his daughters to play tennis—he just insisted that they "do something," even if it was just for fun. Though his oldest daughter did play tennis until she was slowed by an injury, four of his five daughters now play serious golf, and Lendl is reportedly involved every step of the way. Obviously it is not genetic *tennis* skill that put his daughters in the golf ranks, but it is most likely the many other physical and mental skills that a former professional athlete brings to the party and imparts upon offspring. (Lendl is a golf fanatic, himself.)

An *Eastbay.com* blog profile of brothers Kevin Boss (NFL player) and Terry Boss (professional soccer player) describes how they grew up in a small logging town in Oregon and were extremely competitive with each other from a young age. Says Kevin, "We were pretty competitive in everything. We'd be out on the basketball court all hours of the night playing one-on-one and just different sports. ... We both want to win at everything. He [Terry] was the one that was pushing me, being the older brother. When I was coming up in high school, he was always the one to push me."

Sports families also provide emotional support for each other because "they have been there." As a result, a parent or sibling who has played a sport at a high level can give their athlete son/daughter/sibling a clear, healthy perspective on the importance (or lack thereof) of a game, win, or experience. Said basketball player Taurean Green, in talking about his father who played in the NBA: "Just having somebody that played the game and coached the game, it helps just to hear his opinion on just the game of basketball."

The previously mentioned Boss brothers experience the same support, with Terry saying, "It's such a blessing to be able to have a brother that plays pro sports. ... It's so great to have someone so close to you that does what you do day in, day out."

The Matthews family, in particular, warrants a relatively extensive commentary because the three generations of Matthews represent the epitome of a successful sports family. *(Clay, Sr.; sons Clay, Jr. and Bruce; grandsons Clay III, Casey, and Kevin all made it into the NFL.*) In fact, NFL coach Jeff Fisher once told *ESPN.com*; "Whatever they've [the Matthews] got, the family ought to bottle it and sell it, because they'd make a fortune. Whatever it is, it's the right stuff, since that family has certainly set a good example for the NFL for a long time. I'm sure it all gets back to their upbringing. You can see they sure had a solid foundation."

I personally interviewed former NFL star Clay Matthews Jr., and I would like to highlight some of his comments—without turning this section into a Matthews family history.

It is clear, through the Matthews story, that it wasn't necessarily genetics or "football-crazy" parents that took each of the Matthews athletes to their level of accomplishment. In fact, the Matthews' success, throughout each family, is apparently due more to the strong character lessons they were taught as they were growing up—across generations. According to Clay, Jr., his father, Clay, Sr., never talked about football—he talked more in philosophical terms about life lessons. (But, as Clay, Jr. pointed out, those "life lessons" directly apply to sports, as well—so they did have some influence.)

Though Clay, Sr. played professional football in the early 1950s, the game was different back then, and he didn't necessarily think of it as a viable career option for his sons. As Clay, Jr. explained, "The NFL was more of an adventure than a career when Dad played... [The parents] pushed education. There was never anything he [Dad] did that influenced my choice of football." In fact, he says that his father was too busy with his business career and supporting a large family to even be involved in his football. (Clay, Jr's mother wanted him to be a dentist, not a football player.)

When asked why he thinks both he and his younger brother, Bruce, did end up playing professional football, Clay, Jr. thinks that they were probably a little influenced just by the fact that their father played the game, but that he and Bruce were both primarily motivated by the same thing—wanting to be really good at something. Also, he points out that he only chose football (instead of his other high school sport, basketball) because he was better at football.

Though two of his sons, Clay III and Casey, also made it to the NFL, Clay, Jr. insists that he didn't care what sports his kids played when they were growing up. He "just wanted them to be involved in something" and to enjoy sports. In fact, he admits that he was a "little leery" of them pursuing football, and was even reluctant to let them play, because of "all that stress and everything; always being hurt and worrying about an injury." He does acknowledge that his football career may have created a little pressure on the boys to choose football—but it didn't come from him; it more likely came from their friends who expected them to play football because of their dad's NFL career.

Finally ... when asked what he did do that contributed to his kids' level of success in sports, Clay, Jr. replied: "I was patient enough for them to make their decision about what they wanted to do. Once they made that decision, they had the drive to do it. And that's where the drive has to come from."

THEY'RE ONLY HUMAN.

EVEN SUCCESSFUL ATHLETES.......

... make mistakes—even really stupid mistakes.

... have all failed or "collapsed" at one time or another.

... have been nervous—and most still get nervous at times.

... have had injuries—even really stupid injuries.

... are not good at everything athletic or even in their own sport.

... sometimes depend on good luck charms or superstitions.

... aren't as concerned about winning as you might think.

SUCCESSFUL ATHLETES MAKE MISTAKES

Successful athletes make lots of mistakes. As legendary coach John Wooden often said, "If you're not making mistakes, then you're not doing anything. I'm positive that a doer makes mistakes." But the difference between a successful athlete making mistakes and many less successful athletes making mistakes is that *the successful athletes bounce right back from the mistake and don't let it affect their confidence, attitude or playing skills. And successful athletes learn from their mistakes.*

Ironically, it is the fear of making mistakes that is said to be most damaging. That fear makes athletes timid in play, which increases the number and degree of mistakes. According to sports psychologist Bob Rotella, perfectionism in an athlete can be a self-defeating quality because perfectionists can set their standards too high and ultimately get frustrated, angry, and discouraged. Then, they might try even harder—demanding even more of themselves and becoming too self-critical. Eventually athletic performance suffers and the athlete risks depression, anxiety, and lower self- esteem.

Dr. Rotella goes on to explain that this is why it is so important for everyone to recognize that all athletes make mistakes, and that it is the response to those mistakes that makes the difference. This lesson must be learned early on in the athletic experience.

Perhaps the following examples will teach the lesson more effectively than just the preaching of it. A few of the more famous athlete mistakes:

Bill Buckner had a successful 20-year career in Major League Baseball (70's & 80's), but he has become the "go to" name for many (baby boomer) sports fans and announcers whenever they want to refer to a "huge sports mistake."

Specifically, in Game 6 of the 1986 World Series, the Mets scored a winning run against the Boston Red Sox (Buckner's team) when Mookie Wilson hit a "soft" ground ball down the first base line that went clearly underneath the glove and through the legs of Bill Buckner. The Mets went on to win Game 7 and the World Series, and the sports world never, ever, ever let Buckner off the hook.

After all this time, Buckner is still teased about his mistake any time he is recognized, or any time he speaks. Though the continued response has been out-of-proportion to the mistake (some fans might not think so), through the years Buckner has been a good sport about the whole thing and has even portrayed himself in entertainment gags that make fun of it.

Former professional hockey player Steve Smith scored a goal at the wrong end of the ice—a mistake that cost his team, the Edmonton Oilers, an opportunity to go to the Stanley Cup Finals. (They apparently didn't hold it against him—he ended up as coach of the Oilers.)

As described in a *Yahoo!Sports* article, pro baseball pitcher Jhoulys Chacin "muffed" a routine throw from his catcher that allowed the ball to get away, leading to a run scored and a lost game. His very frustrated Rockies manager, Jim Tracy, told the *Denver Post*, "That's a first for me in 11 years [and] it's very difficult for me to take. I don't know what the hell happened." Said broadcaster Chip Caray, "I've never seen that in a major-league game." (The article did point out one other time when that happened—in 2005. It's a rare mistake.)

Retired Minnesota Vikings defensive end Jim Marshall once picked up a fumble and ran 66 yards in the wrong direction to score what he thought would be a touchdown. Not realizing what he had done, he then celebrated by throwing the ball down—scoring an additional safety for his opponents! To make matters worse, this performance was on National TV. Nevertheless, Marshall went back into the game.

Said Marshall, in a "Gridiron Greats" interview; "If you make a mistake, you got to make it right. I realized I had a choice. I could sit in my misery or I could do something about it."

With 18 seconds left in the 1993 Michigan-UNC NCAA basketball title game, Chris Webber called a timeout for Michigan—but Michigan didn't have any more timeouts. As a result, a technical was called on Michigan, and UNC won the game. As tears ran down his face after the game, Webber cried, "I cost our team the game." Nevertheless, his mistake was apparently forgiven—he was the #1 overall NBA draft pick in 1993.

In pro quarterback Dan Orlovsky's first NFL start, he ran out of the back of his own end zone in the first quarter of the game on a 3rd-and-10—and he kept playing, not realizing what he had done. Said Orlovksy to *USA Today*, "When they started blowing the whistle, I was like 'Did we false start or were there offsides or something?' Then I looked and I was like 'You are an idiot.' "

As an indication of how Orlovsky personally handled that humiliating mistake: two years later, a fan posted an autographed photo of Orlovsky online in which Orlovsky signed, "I'm just an idiot."

Former Major League Baseball player Chuck Knoblauch once continued to argue with an umpire while the game was going on and he didn't go after a hit ball like he should have done— allowing a runner to score from first base, and giving the opposing team a 2-1 lead in the 12th inning of the game. And, speaking of Chuck Knoblauch; he also threw an errant ball that hit sports journalist Keith Olbermann's mother, who was sitting seven rows into the stands behind first base.

Former Avalanche hockey goalie Patrick Roy thought he had the puck secure on a goal attempt by the opposing Red Wings in the 2002 Western Conference Finals, so he celebrated with "a pose." But the puck hit the ice during "the pose" and the Red Wings scored. *That didn't prevent Roy from being selected as the greatest goaltender in NHL history in 2004.*

Tim Brown, the first wide receiver to win the Heisman Trophy, fumbled the opening play of his first game as a freshman at Notre Dame. He has since said, "After that I tried to hide, stay in the background. Every time the coaches looked at me I was shaking in my boots." But he credits his coach at Notre Dame, Lou Holtz, with getting him through that stage and building his confidence—all the way to his Heisman.

SOCIAL MEDIA MISTAKES

This category of mistakes deserves its own heading because it is becoming a problem that kids and parents have to learn more about—if for no other reason than to avoid making the same mistakes.

There are many stories of teenagers losing athletic scholarships because of their posts on social media, and I personally heard of a Division I scholarship that was lost when the athlete's future college coach saw unflattering and drunken pictures of him on his Facebook page.

After incriminating pictures from a party were posted on Facebook, Glendbard South High School student-athletes who drank at the party were suspended from participating in part of their athletic seasons. Facing some resistance, the school district defended itself by explaining that they had devised a code of conduct for student-athletes in order to encourage them to be leaders, and they expect them to follow it.

Michigan State took away the football scholarship of new recruit Jay Harris after he posted several "profanity-laced music videos" on YouTube. (Harris then gave up any plans to play college football and decided to try to develop a hip-hop career instead.)

Yuri Wright, a top high school cornerback recruit, was expelled from high school because of sexually graphic and racially insensitive posts he made on Twitter. The official explanation his coach gave *ESPNNewYork.com* was, "We told them [team members] about 10 or 15 times to get off [Twitter] and not to be involved in it, but there is always somebody who thinks he knows better." (In addition, Wright was scheduled to go to Michigan on a recruiting visit, but the school cancelled the visit.)

The varsity baseball team from a suburban Chicago school was forced to forfeit its state playoff games by the school's athletic director after they shared—online—"inappropriate" photos of some of their female classmates. In a letter to parents explaining the decision, the athletic director wrote, "We believe that the complicit behavior of the team and the degradation of fellow female classmates is completely unacceptable ..."

SUCCESSFUL ATHLETES GET NERVOUS

Successful athletes claim to still get nervous before games/competitions—though the nervous feelings usually (but not always) go away once the game starts. Experts consider nerves to be a normal and healthy part of sports, regardless of the level of play, or the age or experience of the athlete; and they tend to agree that an athlete should have some nervousness before a game, or else he/she is likely not fully vested in the game. It is healthier and more productive for any athlete (at any age) to acknowledge and manage nerves than to try to suppress them and pretend that they do not exist. Most athletes also recognize that a certain level of nervousness before any sports competition can be an advantage—because it gets the "juices flowing" and the adrenaline rushing.

Sometimes athletes admit to being "more nervous than usual" when a particular game counts more to them, such as a championship game. For example, baseball star Mark Teixeira told *Sports Illustrated Kids* that when the ball was heading towards him for the last out of the 2009 World Series game he was thinking, "Don't drop it!" Admitted Teixeira, "That was maybe the most nervous I've ever been catching a ball at first base." And even Cy Young Award winner Tim Lincecum admitted he was nervous during the World Series: " ... because it is the World Series. It's a first for a lot of us and a different kind of atmosphere," he explained. (From an article by the Positive Coaching Alliance.)

Baseball superstar Albert Pujols told *SIKids.com* that he gets nervous three times: "*ONE* is my first at-bat of spring training, *TWO* is my first at-bat opening day. And *THIRD* is my first at-bat of the playoffs. If you don't have any pressure and you don't feel like you have that pressure, you aren't ready for the game."

THE "YIPS"

There is another element of "nerves" that happens to successful athletes, and it has never been clear to experts who have studied the phenomena whether it is a mental or a physical issue. (Most agree it is probably a combination of the two.) This condition is technically called *focal dystonia*, but is often referred to as "the yips." Having the yips is a legitimate problem that results in an athlete's loss of fine motor skills—without an apparent explanation. Sometimes the suffering athlete recovers from the problem, sometimes he/she adjusts their techniques to deal with it, and sometimes a case of the yips will cause an athlete to give up a sport completely.

The yips can happen in any sport, and there are many well-known examples. In golf, a Mayo clinic study claims that 33-48% of all serious golfers have experienced the yips—which cause a golfer to jerk and twitch during a putting attempt. In fact legendary golfer Ben Hogan suffered from the yips, as have Bernhard Langer, Sam Snead, Harry Vardon ... to name just a few.

The yips tend to affect basketball players when they are at the free throw line, they affect tennis players typically when serving, and football players most commonly experience the yips when kicking a field goal. In baseball, the yips result in the inability to throw the ball accurately, with the throwing arm twitching or jerking with the release of the ball. (In baseball, this problem has also been referred to as "Steve Blass Disease" or "Steve Sax Syndrome" because each of those players also suffered the same problem—along with others such as Mackey Sasser and Rick Ankiel.)

One of the more well-known cases of the yips in baseball is the problem experienced by Chuck Knoblauch. At one time, Knoblauch was considered one of the best fielders in baseball, but he began having difficulty making accurate throws to first base. The problem persisted, so he had to be moved to different positions to compensate. (Maybe that's why he hit Keith Olbermann's mother...)

SUCCESSFUL ATHLETES GET INJURED IN CARELESS AND UNEXPECTED WAYS

(Make sure your kids read this section so they will maybe think before they act......)

Baseball pitcher Joel Zumaya missed game action because of a sore wrist he developed from playing too much "Guitar Hero" on Playstation.

Baseball's Rickey Henderson fell asleep on an ice pack and got frostbite, which forced him to miss three games.

Former NFL quarterback Gus Frerotte scored in an important game and intentionally slammed his head into the pylon padding (in celebration)—spraining his neck so badly that he had to go to the hospital. (He missed the rest of the overtime, tie game.)

NFL kicker Bill Gramatica kicked a 43 yard field goal and jumped for joy, but landed so poorly that he tore his ACL. Said Gramatica after the injury, "My jump was excellent. It was my landing I needed to work on. It was funny. It was part of my career. I talk about it all the time. You have to laugh about it."

NBA player Tony Allen played through the whistle of a game, dunked, missed the shot and fell—tearing his ACL and missing the rest of the season as a result. Said Allen, "I watch it every day. Every day. Like when I go back home, I'll watch it all the way up until that point. I had 19 points."

Baseball pitcher Steve Sparks dislocated his shoulder while in the minor leagues when he tried to rip a phone book in half after watching a motivational training session.

Former NFL player Robert Pratt pulled a hamstring while heading to midfield for the coin toss.

Baseball player Kendrys Morales celebrated his Grand Slam by jumping on home plate, landing the wrong way, and breaking his lower leg. He missed the rest of the 2010 season and all of the 2011 season because of the injury.

Seattle Seahawks defensive end Red Bryant was celebrating a safety in a game while he was on the sidelines—without a helmut—and chest bumped a teammate who did have a helmut on ... chipping a tooth.

The NBA's Kyrie Irving broke his hand by smacking a padded wall after a frustrating turnover at practice.

Pitcher Joba Chamberlain dislocated his ankle when he was jumping on a trampoline with his son.

Hockey player Marian Gaborik was out of action due to a "lower bodily injury" from a game of hacky sak.

Baseball star Chris Coghlan tore the meniscus in his knee while hitting a teammate in the face with a pie in celebration of a victory.

First overall NHL draft pick Erik Johnson injured his ACL when he got his foot stuck while getting out of a golf cart—before his first appearance in a league game. The game of golf also left NHL star Claude Giroux needing surgery on his finger after his golf club shattered and splintered into his index finger. (Johnson tweeted Giroux: "Hey @28Giroux, don't worry it happens bro. #buddies")

Amar'e Stoudemire sliced his hand punching a fire extinguisher glass case after a playoff loss.

"Tampa Rays' Reliever Joel Peralta Injures Neck Getting Sandwich" (Saw this headline, but have to admit that I didn't read the article.)

Basketball pro Vladimir Radmanovic separated his shoulder trying to snowboard for the first time—even though it was in violation of his contract.

And yet another "angry punching" injury: MLB infielder Sean Rodriguez broke his right hand while punching a locker after being told he would be sent down to a minor league team for a short time.

Professional soccer player Alan Wright had to exchange his new Ferrari when he realized that using the gas pedal was injuring his knee.

Former baseball star Wade Boggs missed 6 games as a result of crashing into the arm of a couch in his hotel room while trying to take off his cowboy boots.

The NFL's LaRon Landry reportedly "limped" through his first professional mini-camp after being hit in the groin during a game of paintball.

Marty Cordova, former Major League baseball player, fell asleep in a tanning bed and had to stay out of the sun— missing a game.

Former MLB pitcher Adam Eaton used a knife to open a DVD and accidentally stabbed himself in the stomach.

Disclaimer: *Most of these anecdotes were found on websites, ThePostgame.com; Yahoo!Sports; and BleacherReport.com; I can't confirm that all of the injuries happened exactly the way they are described....*

SUCCESSFUL ATHLETES ARE NOT GOOD AT EVERYTHING AND ARE NOT GOOD ALL THE TIME

Kids need to understand at a young age that no athlete is good at everything, and that most successful athletes are not good at all the requirements of their sport, either. Though there are athletes who are considered great "all-around players" or "5-tool players" (as they say in baseball), most (if not all) of those five-tool-players would probably admit they still have strengths and weaknesses.

According to a *Los Angeles Times* article, Chase Utley's batting made him a first round pick in the 2000 draft, and his glove has made him the best all-around second baseman in baseball. However, according to the *Times* profile, Utley struggled for years to master baseball's simplest task—throwing the ball.

By the same token, even the really great athletes aren't great at what they do all the time. They have good days and bad days, just like every other real-world human. Following are some supporting examples:

Quarterback Tom Brady told *Sports Illustrated Kids,* "Growing up, I can remember kids who were faster than me and kids who were better jumpers than me. I wasn't going to beat them on pure athletic ability. So I found other ways. I realized I didn't have to run for 10 yards. I can throw it to somebody and let him run for 10 yards."

Somebody in the NFL has to be the one to have "the most fumbles in a season," but those players typically keep their jobs because they are great at another aspect of football. For example, David Wilson had the most fumbles in 2013; Philip Rivers had the most in 2012; Blaine Gabbert had the most in 2011.

By the same token, somebody in the NBA has to have the lowest free throw percentage each year, but those players generally keep their jobs, as well. These greats of the NBA were notorious for their bad free-throw shooting: Shaquille O'Neal, Wilt Chamberlain, Bill Russell ... to name just a few.

In a slightly different vein, there are successful athletes who were extremely good and extremely bad at seemingly similar skills. (That's what happens when you *GO FOR IT*......) For example:

Dave Kingman twice led the National League in home runs—but batted a .236 average and led the league in "whiffs" three times.

Reggie Jackson, one of the best baseball players in the league when he played, hit 563 home runs and stole 228 bases in his career—though he also had a record 2597 strikeouts in 2820 games.

Former quarterback great Brett Favre was the only quarterback to throw for over 70,000 yards and 500 touchdowns, and was the only player to win MVP three times in a row. But he also had 336 interceptions and the most career fumbles of any quarterback.

Baseball pitching legend Nolan Ryan retired with a .526 winning percentage—but he also was responsible for the most walks ever by a pitcher.

There was a fairly well-known NIKE commercial featuring former NBA great Michael Jordan, in which Jordan points out; "I've missed more than 9,000 shots in my career. I've lost almost 300 games. Twenty-six times I've been trusted to take the game winning shot and missed. I've failed over and over again in my life. And that is why I succeed."

Baseball Hall of Famer Jim Rice had 28 home runs and 122 RBIs, but ... he also set a record for grounding into double plays.

Even though baseball great Rickey Henderson set a record by stealing 1406 bases during his career ... he also set the record for getting caught trying to steal.

Ben Wallace had a long, 16-year career in the NBA—even though he had the worst free throw percentage in NBA history (41.4%).

Mark Reynolds is known in Major League Baseball for his power-hitting. But he also had the record for the most whiffs in a season, and he holds the all-time record for the most strikeouts in a season.

Former NBA player Tim Hardaway had an extremely successful career, but still holds the NBA record for "worst single game shooting performance"—0 for 17 from the floor.

Though NFL Hall of Famer Troy Aikman was a superstar quarterback and #1 draft pick, he lost the first 11 games he started in the NFL.

Finally ... highly respected baseball instructor Steve Hayward was asked in an interview; *If you had your playing career to do over, what would you do differently?* and he replied, " ... I would have been more forgiving of myself when I failed. I thought I had to be perfect every at bat. I just never thought about good hitters making an out 7 out of 10 times. I thought I should hit the ball hard every time up and it just made the game not as fun for me."

SOME SUCCESSFUL ATHLETES HAVE SUPERSTITIONS/ QUIRKS/RITUALS

Some of you parents have already had experience with your kids' personal superstitions or quirks, whether they be sports-related or not. You might have even argued with your kids or your spouse about how to approach this issue. It is important for you and your kids to know, however, that this aspect of childhood is very common, in general, and it is also common for kids to have superstitions or rituals that are associated with playing sports.

And it is not just the kids who have sports-related superstitions! Parents sometimes do, too. In fact, a McDavid and SSI survey of 1,000 adults (published in *USA TODAY*) indicated that *31% of parents claim to wear a lucky t-shirt to their kids' game; 24% say they recite a special saying or song before a game; and 23% say they prepare a special pre-game dinner.*

This is a conflicted topic because there are polar opposite opinions among sports psychology experts about the impact of these rituals/supersitions on young, and older, athletes' performance. Some youth sports psychologists point out that, while it is common for young athletes to have superstitions, having them can negatively impact their confidence: he/she might attribute too much power to the superstition and might be emotionally crippled without it.

On the other hand, there are other youth (and adult) sports experts who feel that these rituals and habits actually work the other way—they give the athlete confidence and security. So, here again, parents have to make their own decision as to how to handle the issue, on an individual basis.

It is worth noting, nevertheless, that there are many successful athletes who "are said to have" these types of habits and/or superstitions, but have still flourished in the world of competitive sports—either in spite of the superstition, or because of it. For example:

The great Michael Jordan "is said to have" worn his University of North Carolina shorts under his Bulls NBA uniform for every game.

"It has been said that" tennis great Serena Williams ties her shoelaces a specific way; bounces the ball five times before her first serve, and twice before her second serve; and wears the same pair of socks for an entire tournament.

Baseball Hall of Famer Wade Boggs "is said to have"... eaten chicken before every game; always taken batting practice at the same time every day; and drawn the word "Chai" (Hebrew for "life") in the dirt before going to bat.

Former baseball pro Kevin Rhomberg "is said to have" had to touch someone back if they touched him. (Others players used this quirk against him—often.)

"It has been said" that Hall of Fame NHL goaltender Patrick Roy was known for talking to the net posts during games; he never talked to reporters on game days; he wouldn't let his skates touch the lines on the ice; he wrote his children's names on his sticks before each game ... (and those are just what sportswriters know about.)

NBA player Jason Terry (described as "the most superstitious player in the NBA" by *Men's Health* magazine) "is said to" eat chicken before games and wear five pairs of socks while playing. Also, the night before a game he wears the shorts of the next day's opposing team when he goes to bed.

SUCCESSFUL ATHLETES AREN'T ALL ABOUT JUST WINNING

The benefits of kids learning to win and lose in a healthy way through youth sports was addressed briefly in an earlier chapter, but it is worth pointing out, again, that successful athletes don't necessarily focus specifically on the concept of *winning* games in their sports lives; they focus on the process of *playing,* and the level to which they, themselves, are playing. By all accounts, it takes this mentality to truly succeed in sports. The goal of winning is secondary to the goal of performing at a peak level as often as possible.

Though, of course, winning is the end "goal" of competitive activity, successful athletes in *team* sports recognize that winning is not under the control of any one athlete, so they can't worry about it. All they can worry about is their own performance and hope the team plays well together.

In competitive *individual* sports, as well, athletes tend to accept that winning is not under their control because they can only control how they perform—not how their competition performs. So they focus on the process and they strive for a high level of performance, without necessarily thinking specifically about "winning," or producing a record-setting performance.

For example:

After qualifying for professional golf's U.S. Open as the second youngest qualifier, 16-year-old Beau Hossler said, "I was thinking about playing the best I could, not qualifying for the U.S. Open."

Eric Heiden, a speed skater who won a sweep of five gold medals in the 1980 Olympics, explained, "I never once thought about the consequences or legacy of my efforts. A perfect Olympics never entered my consideration."

Even coach Vince Lombardi, who provided the sports world with one of the most frequently quoted phrases about winning— *Winning isn't everything; it's the only thing*—has claimed that this quote has been misinterpreted. According to sports psychologist Dr. Bob Rotella (whose brother was friends with Lombardi), Lombardi was actually referring to the *commitment* to winning and the *commitment* to excellence; he saw winning as an attitude and a state of mind, rather than an end result.

As Rotella explains in his book, *The Golfer's Mind*, Lombardi's specific explanation (to Rotella's cousin Sal) of the meaning behind the phrase was that "sometimes his teams might lose a game by a touchdown or two, but if he thought the team had made the commitment and given it their best, he would be the first to pat them on the back in the locker room and tell them what a great job they did. On the other hand, there might be times when he felt they were the better team and they lost because they didn't give a full commitment and their best effort. Then, he'd be the first to kick them in the butt and tell them so."

Another perspective: After reading an article in *USA Today* about "Jock Culture," a reader named Rick Burns, a college soccer coach for 26 years, wrote a very touching and insightful letter back to the newspaper in response. Parts of his letter follow: *When I connect with my former players, I often hear them reminisce about moments—not records...Ultimately, I found that winning is overrated, and that the singular quest for it leads only to unhappiness. My experience made it clear that the joy of victory fades immediately... Over the years, two things became more important than results for me—that my players enjoyed their experience and that they fought the good fight on the field."*

Along that same line of thinking: Former NFL player Billy Miller told the *Ventura County Star* that high school days were some of the greatest of his life but, "It never was about winning games and winning championships. It's about getting together with your friends on a Friday night and seeing how well we could play as a team."

When talking about winning, the concept of "perfection" often comes up, particularly in sports with ratings such as gymnastics. And while there are so-called "perfect scores" or "perfect seasons," many successful athletes insist that they don't think in terms of perfection; instead, they think about performing the best that they can. Sportswriter Bill Pennington discussed the concept of perfection in sports in a *New York Times* article, and referred to the following two athletes, specifically:

As gymnast Nadia Comaneci said of getting her "perfect 10" score at the 1976 Olympics; "During my routine and even after it, I did not think it was all that perfect. I thought it was pretty good, but athletes don't think about history when making history. They think about what they're doing, and that's how it gets done." She also insists that she did not even look at the scoreboard at the end of her routine until her teammates started pointing toward it.

As explained by the leader of the 35-0 Connecticut women's 1994-95 championship basketball team, "I can assure you that we never talked about being undefeated. It was something that happened on the way to a championship."

Finally ... The great and legendary UCLA coach John Wooden had his own thoughts about winning and perfection. Said Wooden, "There is no perfect season. You can have a season where you win all your games. But that is far from perfect." He also claimed, *"I never even mentioned trying to win games to my teams.* I did talk about perfection. I said it was not possible, but I said it's not impossible to try for it. That's what we did in every practice and game." (Wooden also insisted that players focus on playing the best basketball with each possession and wait until the end of the game to look at the score.)

FEMALES AND SPORTS

An Indiana University study of athletic performance in children showed that, until roughly around the ages of 12–13, there is very little difference in athletic performance between boys and girls. But boys' bodies and girls' bodies go in acutely different directions once puberty hits, and that is where the competitive gap begins.

Females have more opportunities in youth sports than they have ever had, and they are taking advantage of their opportunities in huge numbers. For example, the 2012 Summer Olympics highlighted the fact that American women are succeeding in a cross-section of sports, with 56% of the United States medals won by women, and 66% of the US gold medals won by women.

There is no question that girls benefit from youth sports participation in much the same way that boys do. Research indicates that girls in sports are healthier overall, and they are less likely to smoke, get pregnant, or use drugs and alcohol than girls who do not participate in sports. They are also more likely to stay in school, and their social skills are said to be more developed. Studies reported in *Sports Illustrated* also show that female high school athletes are more likely than non-athletic girls to do well in science classes.

Since body image is of particular concern to most young girls, the Women's Sports Foundation has made a concerted effort to show young girls that real-world successful female athletes "come in all shapes and sizes." And, says Amy Parlapiano of *ThePostGame.com,* "Many successful female athletes develop confidence in their body image from sports. They've [female athletes] learned how to embrace who they are and take what they have, take something that someone else might consider a flaw, and use that to further their game."

Olympic swimming medalist Missy Franklin had difficulty dealing with the fact that she was "a head above everyone in her grade," but swimming made her see what an advantage her height was. Said Franklin, "I realized it [height] was a gift. It helped me succeed at what I love to do. And so I grew to absolutely love it now. It's just the best. I wish I were even taller."

Also addressing body image, soccer star Alex Morgan claimed that soccer taught her to love herself. "It's important for women to feel confident in their own body, whether they have broad shoulders or big calves, or whatever," says Morgan. "I have big calves and I love showing off my legs because of it. So whether your body is athletic or skinny or big-boned, it doesn't matter. You should love it no matter what."

Girls are even participating, to some extent, on boys' teams. Though not an overwhelming trend, there are girls like Andrea Marsh, of Panama, New York, who played for 9 years on a boys' football team and led the league in interceptions her senior year. (She was even named a team captain.) And Erin Dimeglio, who saw playing time as a third-string quarterback for her varsity high school football team, played quarterback for the high school flag football team, and played on the girls' basketball team.

But then there are also girls like Angela Ruggiero, a 4-time Olympic ice hockey medalist, who says that she was cut from a boys' all-star hockey team at the age of 9 because "they didn't want a girl playing with them." Nevertheless, Angela said that even the experience of getting cut from the boys' team made her a better player because it made her more determined.

Another key difference between boys and girls playing youth sports is the fact that girls reportedly drop out of sports at twice the rate of boys by age 14—for a variety of reasons. In a column about this issue (on their website, *youthsportspsychology.com*), Dr. Patrick and Lisa Cohn refer to work that Dr. Joan Steidenger has done with girls in sports. Dr. Steidenger explains that the reason girls drop out of sports at such a high rate is that, "It's all about their relationships." She adds, "Young women often feel pressure from boyfriends and friends to spend less time playing sports and more time being social ... It becomes a time issue."

NOTE: The Cohns' website provides many suggestions for parents regarding this issue. Also, if you have a daughter in sports, you might be interested in looking into the Women's Sports Foundation, which, among many other projects, has run a public service campaign called Keep Her In the Game—a program designed to encourage girls to stay with sports longer. (See Appendix)

TITLE IX (*Title Nine*)

Girls' sports participation is generally taken for granted now, so it must be difficult for females under the age of about 50 to even imagine that, before 1972, girls in most schools had little athletic opportunity outside of gym class. Back in the "old days," the few female athletes that actually did succeed did so with very little support and acceptance. For example, in 1973, *50,000 men received some form of athletic college scholarship, and only 50 women received college scholarship aid.* And because women's athletic accomplishments were not promoted in the media, successful female athletes in the 1970's and even the 1980's point out that they grew up following male sports

Starting in the 1972-1973 school year, *Title IX* dramatically changed the world of youth sports and, eventually, college and professional sports. However, many don't know much about *Title IX* because the subject doesn't necessarily come up in the everyday sports world anymore. (The 2012 Olympics did highlight it, in celebration of its impact on the sports world.)

So ... in a nutshell ...

Title IX is a law that was passed in 1972 that stated: No person in the United States shall, on the basis of sex, be excluded from participation in, be denied the benefits of or be subjected to discrimination under any education program or activity receiving federal financial assistance.

Most people are surprised to learn that *Title IX* is not specifically about sports—it is about education, opportunity, and equal rights. But *Title IX* is most often referred to in the context of women and sports, as it requires any schools that receive Federal funds to provide equal sports opportunities for women and men.

As a result of *Title IX*, thousands of sports teams have been created for women; the number of females participating in high school athletics has grown from 295,000 to over 3,000,000; and the number of female college athletes has increased from 30,000 to 190,000. (There are even more than 8,000 girls playing on high school ice hockey teams now, compared to only 96 in 1973.)

In an enlightening *Sports Illustrated* article about *Title IX*, expert Donna Loprano claimed that the "fathers of girls led the revolution on the ground" after *Title IX* because "they understood how much sport gave children. Dad was the one who took his daughter into the backyard to play catch. Mom would have, but because she'd never had the chance to play, she didn't understand how much it meant."

Not everyone considers *Title IX* to be "the great salvation," however. The NCAA, for example, actively fought *Title IX*. There are also those who agree, in concept, with *Title IX*, but not with the specific details; and there are some who feel that *Title IX* has resulted in a fairly strong bias toward female athletes and female college scholarships—at the expense of male participation. Said Carrie Lukas, a conservative thought-leader and current Director of the Independent Women's Forum, (in a *U.S. News & World Report* article): "When *Title IX* was enacted, it was meant to open doors for women, not close them for men. But, unfortunately, many men's sports have been negatively affected by the requirements of *Title IX*. Men's sports such as track and field, swimming, and gymnastics have been sacrificed to meet the ever-increasing imbalance of gender in college sports. In 1980, there were 80 men's NCAA gymnastics teams. Today there are fewer than 20."

SUCCESSFUL ATHLETES WHO OVERCAME PHYSICAL AND MENTAL CHALLENGES

(This is a great chapter to share with your kids.)

The following is a poem written by Anthony Robles, an NCAA individual wrestling champion who was born with only one leg. Robles recited his poem when he accepted the Jimmy V Award —an award for perseverance—at the "2011 ESPY Awards":

Every Soul who comes to earth with a leg or two at birth
Must wrestle his opponents knowing,
It's not what is,
But what can be that measures worth.
Make it hard, just make it possible.
And through pain, I won't complain.
My Spirit is unconquerable.
Fearless I will face each foe
For I know I am capable.
I don't care what's probable,
Through blood, sweat and tears,
I am unstoppable.

Anthony Robles has received many other awards, and has been inducted into the National Wrestling Hall of Fame. He is now a motivational speaker and supports the efforts of Team Unstoppable, an organization that "seeks to enable individuals with disabilities to experience freedom through sports and recreation."

This chapter puts the real world of sports into perspective for all the parents of kids (and the kids, themselves) playing sports with completely healthy bodies—two legs, two arms, healthy lungs, a strong heartbeat, and mental clarity. This chapter is also included so that the parents of children with special needs, and the kids, themselves, may be motivated by these real stories. Anyone can see that athletic participation is a viable option with huge rewards!

I can't encourage parents enough to consider getting special needs kids involved in sports—any sport. *Research shows that youth with physical disabilities who participate in physical activity are healthier, more successful in school and have an enhanced quality of life.* (And you, as parents, will also get so much out of it if you get involved yourselves.)

There are special needs youth sports programs in many communities, and there are opportunities to participate in the mainstream programs, as well. There is the well-known Special Olympics program, and there is also The Paralympic Experience, which is a program that is designed to encourage physical fitness and overall well-being in children with disabilities.

AYSO, the presiding organization for the very popular youth soccer programs, also has a program for children with special needs that is called the VIP Program. But, as is probably true with any special needs sports program, AYSO claims that it faces challenges in getting enough volunteers, and that it has difficulty getting the already exhausted, overwhelmed or over-protective parents to be proactive in expanding the choice of activities for their children.

There is also an International Paralympics program for accomplished athletes with disabilities that operates in conjunction with the International Olympics. (Many organizations are listed in the Appendix of this book, and there are other programs that can be found with some "googling.")

In a commentary on *Forbes.com* entitled "A Watershed Moment For Disabled Athletes," well-known sports agent Leigh Steinberg highlights a major change occurring for disabled youth in this country, and emphasizes the positive impact the change will have on disabled kids who want to play sports. Explains Steinberg; "The Department of Education sent a letter telling school administrators that they must afford qualified students with disabilities an equal opportunity for participation in sports. This means that there needs to be equality of opportunity, not results. More conventionally talented students still will win the roster spots in sports. But schools need to provide 'reasonable modifications' to give athletes with disabilities a chance."

Steinberg goes on to describe how schools might end up providing "separate but equal" competitions. Competitive wheel chair basketball, football, and handball opportunities can be provided; and if a school does not have enough disabled athletes to field a team, teams can be formed that are within the same district. "While these letters to schools may not have the same effect as laws," says Steinberg, "they will send a clear message. They put schools on notice that they cannot simply deprive disabled students of the opportunity to compete. It has the potential to have an impact similar to what Title IX did for opportunities for female athletes."

Steinberg finishes with, "Students with disabilities already face enough cruel stereotypes and bullying. They are capable and talented young people with much to offer the world. This crack in the 'disability ceiling' will do these youngsters and the society a world of good."

One example of a proactive school sports program for special needs kids is that of Taft High School in Southern California, which was designated by the school district as the school where deaf and hard-of-hearing students in the district would attend. The high school has used athletics as a way for the deaf students to more easily become a part of the school community; they are encouraged to play football and basketball, and to run cross country and track. The longer the program goes on, the more kids there are participating in sports because they are inspired by the others who are like them and are involved, having fun, and succeeding. (The school also provides a sign language interpreter who works alongside the athletes.)

A story I want you to share with you is one that sportswriter Bill Plaschke wrote about in the *Los Angeles Times* about the Balboa VIP Basketball League for special needs kids.

In the Balboa league, special needs kids from 10 – 18 years of age play basketball games of "7 on 7"—in 5 minute shifts; and, in these games, writes Plaschke, "the referees shrug and smile, the kids rebound in front of the basket, and everyone surrounds them and chants their name until they shoot and score." Every player scores in these basketball games, and the players generously pass the ball to anyone who hasn't scored. Then, at the end of the "tied-score game" that Plaschke was personally watching, "the parents rushed the floor, exchanged high fives and snapped photos." (In order to provide the requisite post-game quote, Plaschke interviewed a 17-year-old player who exclaimed, "I feel like I'm at home here. This is one place I can be myself.")

The story behind the start of the league is ... the league founder, Steve Sisken, has two children who are not special needs children. But when he was coaching his son on a local youth team, a sister of one of his team's players had Down's Syndrome and she kept showing up to practices and asking when it was her time to play. So Sisken invited her and her friends to scrimmage against the team, and word spread. The league developed from there.

Said one parent involved in the league, "Coach Steve is an absolutely amazing guy who is doing this for no other reason than the goodness of his heart. Not once does he treat them like they have special needs. He embraces them for who they are." And the remarkable Steve Sisken enthusiastically pointed out to Bill Plaschke, "I would rather be here than at a Laker game."

One of the more well-known and inspirational professional athletes, Jim Abbott, was born with a disability, but still had incredible success in Major League Baseball. Abbott was born without a right hand, but he still managed to make it to the big leagues as a pitcher. (He was also quarterback of his high school football team and was named Best Amateur Athlete in the country while in college.)

According to a biography of Abbott on the *SABR.org* website, Jim showed an interest in sports at an early age, and his parents always encouraged him to try things. Said his father in a *USA Today* interview; "We decided that if Jim wanted to [play sports] then to let him try. I helped out with some things. But in the end it was all Jim. It had to be." His parents did try to steer him toward a sport like soccer that wouldn't require the use of his hands, but Jim wanted to play baseball because the other kids in the neighborhood were playing baseball. Practicing drills over and over and over again so that he could make his legendary "glove transition move," Abbott perfected his abilities with nothing but extremely hard work and determination.

Regardless of his remarkable feats, Abbott had to face skeptics at every level of accomplishment because of his perceived disability, but he obviously proved the skeptics wrong. As he has often stated, "I've learned that it's not the disability that defines you. It's how you deal with the challenges the disability presents you with." Now Abbott takes pride in inspiring children who have deformities through his many personal efforts.

Kevin Laue has no left hand or left arm below the elbow, and he says he was told all his young life that he couldn't play sports because of his disability—even though he was always quite tall and ended up being 6'11". But he idolized pitcher Jim Abbott and told himself; "If Jim Abbott could pitch for the Yankees with one arm, I could play sports too."

Though Laue had the height of a basketball player, he didn't make the 7th grade basketball team. But instead of giving up, he practiced all summer. By the time 8th grade tryouts came around, Laue was dunking and palming the ball with skills that put him firmly on the team—and he continued to impress throughout high school.

No different than many high school basketball players, Laue's dream was to play Division I basketball, but there were no Division I scholarship offers made. So he went to Fork Union Military Academy and played basketball there—and excelled. In fact, he played so well that he got the attention of the coach at Division I Manhattan College and was offered a spot on that team. Says Kevin, "Maybe me playing with one hand inspires others to try to work harder toward their goals or their dreams."

As a matter of fact, Laue's story is so inspirational that a documentary was made about him entitled: *Long Shot: The Kevin Laue Story.*

Butch Lumpkin was one of the many so-called "Thalidomide Babies" who were born with deformities, and he has what he calls "short arms"—though he basically has no functional arms at all, according to his profile on the website butchlumpkin.com. Nevertheless, with determination and a competitive spirit, he played soccer and tennis as a teen and into his college years, and he followed his tennis passion after college. But always ready to take on a challenge, he decided to play golf when someone mentioned that "golf would be impossible for a man like [him]."

Now, by all accounts, Lumpkin is a great golfer, and he has chosen to travel around the country performing demonstrations in order to show people that nothing's beyond reach if a person sets their mind to it. He has also established the Nothing's Beyond Reach Foundation. (See Appendix)

An athlete who overcame the potential limitations of diabetes is Adam Morrison, the third overall pick in the 2006 NBA draft. Diagnosed with Type 1 Diabetes when he was in 8th grade, he was determined to continue playing basketball, the game that he had already grown to love. But as a teenager, and as a professional athlete, he had to have strong discipline to protect his health, because he would even have to inject himself with insulin during games.

Morrison also has pointed out that former NBA player Chris Dudley was a tremendous inspiration to him, since Dudley was a diabetic and had a 16 year career in the NBA. Said Morrison, in *Diabetes Health Magazine*: "His [Dudley's] example helped me clear up some of the myths and questions I had about what it was going to be like playing with diabetes."

Diagnosed with cerebral palsy as a premature infant, Cortney Jordan walks with a limp, has constant back pain, and is unable to feel the left side of her body. But that didn't stop her from winning a gold medal in swimming at the Paralympic Games. Said Cortney in a *Thousand Oaks Acorn* article; "When I'm in the pool, I don't feel pain. It's the only place where I don't feel pain." She added, "Swimming has been great for my life. It has given me a lot more strength and usage of my body."

Cortney did admit that she was very discouraged when she first started swimming, because she was competing against able-bodied swimmers. But then she discovered the Paralympics and thrived.

Former professional baseball player Curtis Pride was born deaf, but he was able to accomplish a great deal in baseball, even though, as he told *USA Today*, "Deafness is a challenge to a baseball player when it comes to hearing the ball off the bat, catching flies and throwing to cut off men."

Now coaching baseball at Gallaudet University, a school for the deaf and hard of hearing, he claims that it isn't easy to find deaf baseball players "because the good ones are being recruited by Division I & II teams."

Speaking of Gallaudet University ... A *Parade Magazine* article about the women's basketball team there that is made up of deaf or hard-of-hearing players, describes how they ended their 2011 season with a 23-2 record in a conference where they were the only non-hearing team.

Though the teammates quite effectively communicate with each other through head nods, hand motions, and mouth movements, the team's coach speculates that they lose at least 6 points a game because they are looking at one another. But he also admits that the team has an advantage over the hearing teams that they play against because those teams can't understand the players' hand signals.

Losing all of her hearing her sophomore year in high school, after being hard of hearing since birth, Emily Cressy commented on her opportunity to play college soccer at the University of Kansas, and how it "keeps her sane." Said Emily in *USA Today*, "It's my life. It makes me feel like I'm not deaf when I'm on the field. Like I'm just a normal human being."

Derrick Coleman, Jr. has been deaf since birth but he didn't let that stop him from excelling in sports throughout his childhood, and ultimately playing football on a scholarship for UCLA. In an article written by Mike Trudell, Coleman's mother explained that "Derrick was always very, very, very active. He needed a sport to play." And since Derrick had an affinity for football, and had a body made to play football, his parents allowed him to play. (His mother also explained how she protected Derrick's hearing aids: "I put a pair of my pantyhose over them to keep them secure in his helmut.")

Derrick's high school friend and teammate also told Trudell, "When you get to know him [Coleman], you realize his athleticism only got him so far. The reason he is so good and continuing to play at a high level is because of his hearing — because he had to work three times as hard as anyone on the field ... If he weren't deaf, I don't think he'd be nearly as powerful — emotionally or physically."

Hall of Fame MLB player Jim Eisenreich experienced the symptoms of Tourette's Syndrome as a child (facial tics, making noises, etc), but his condition was not diagnosed until he was an adult, and after he began a career playing Major League Baseball.

Starting in childhood, sports became an extremely important part of Eisenreich's coping with his condition, and he has said that despite the behaviors he displayed as a child, and the teasing of some of his schoolmates, he was accepted on the sports field by his friends and teammates. "Sports was my outlet for a lot of my problems," said Eisenreich. "I was accepted there. My friends were OK with that. I was OK with that."

Eisenreich stood out throughout high school and college as a skilled baseball player, and he ultimately made it to the pros. But as he struggled quite publicly with tics that were, at that time, considered to be the result of "a case of nerves," mocking and taunting from fans forced Eisenreich to take a disability leave to deal with his condition—which had still not been diagnosed. Once Tourette's Syndrome was diagnosed, however, Eisenreich had the courage to go back to professional baseball when he was given another chance—and he excelled.

Eisenreich's continued strength and determination led to several awards that recognized the fact that he overcame such a significant obstacle—one of which was his team's Player of the Year award. He has since created The Jim Eisenreich Foundation for Children with Tourette Syndrome. (See Appendix)

Another very successful athlete who has not let Tourette's Syndrome stop him is professional soccer player Tim Howard, who was diagnosed in the 6th grade. Despite his Tourette's symptoms, he starred in both soccer and basketball in high school, and went on to become one of the great goalkeepers in

Major League Soccer. Howard has also discussed the positive impact of sports on his condition, explaining that he immersed himself in sports while growing up, and that being on a sports field made his tics less noticable to others.

A fair number of successful athletes have also been very open and candid about their struggles with ADD/ADHD, particularly as it relates to their sports careers. These athletes like to stress to kids and parents that the symptoms can be controlled, with or without medication. They also insist that these kids can succeed in sports.

MLB first baseman Adam LaRoche has often talked about how his game and his stats improved once he got his ADHD under control with medication. Others, such as baseball's Tom Gorzelanny, Derek Lowe, and Scott Eyre have been open about their experiences, and have been encouraging, as well.

Star baseball player Shane Victorino's biography describes how he was diagnosed with ADD/ADHD at an early age, and that sports was an outlet for his energy. In the book, Shane's mother explains, "As Shane got older he learned how to manage and cope with his ADHD. My husband and I looked at it not as a disability but as a challenge. When he played, he always played with intensity, and we're so proud of how he channeled his energy and focus."

An article written by Judy Dutton in *ADDitude* magazine talks about the fact that many successful athletes who have been diagnosed with ADD/ADHD have claimed that playing sports as kids, and as adults, has helped them focus—even though they had difficulty focusing on academics. (Some have used medication and some haven't.)

Experts have long believed that sports such as baseball and golf might not be appropriate sports for kids with ADD/ADHD, because those sports require a great deal of concentration and focus. But baseball's Tom Gorzelanny voices his disagreement with the theory that baseball is not a good sport for kids with ADD/ADHD. (He succeeds in spite of it.) In a *USA Today* article about the subject, he specifically tells kids with ADD/ADHD: "Find something you have interest in. If you love something, then you should definitely do it. If it's playing baseball or basketball or golf and you know you can focus on it, then you should do it. That could be your medicine."

To add to that, Adam LaRoche expresses concern that an ADD/ADHD diagnosis might hold some kids back, saying, "I don't want it to hinder kids, have them thinking they can't make it in sports or prevent them from becoming astronauts or policemen. It's something very painless to deal with. Don't be ashamed to see somebody about it. Don't be embarrassed. If I'm not embarrassed on a national level, then they shouldn't be."

Anjali Forber-Pratt became paralyzed from the waist down as a very young child, but she describes that fate on her website as "a positive life-altering event" that gave her "an innate drive and determination that she has utilized in every facet of her life." She took this drive to the sports world after attending a sports clinic for children with disabilities at the age of 5, and by the age of 9 years old she was competing at the national level in track and field (wheelchair racing). After some track injuries, however, she was forced to switch sports, so she began an award-winning downhill skiing career—and eventually went back to track, as well.

Now, as an adult, Forber-Pratt has become a strong advocate for kids with disabilities to participate in sports, and has written a book called *Color, Learn & Play*. The book is designed to encourage young children with disabilities to play sports, and to educate young aspiring Paralympians on the variety of sports they can play.

Jonathan Stoklosa, a champion weight lifter in the Special Olympics, was born with Downs Syndrome. Though doctors told his father early on, "He's not going to be able to do anything," Stoklosa began lifting weights at age 12 with his two older brothers, and by the age of 16 he had set records in competition. In addition, he wrestled for four years in high school and graduated.

Charlotte Brown is a legally blind teenager in Texas who plays on the school basketball team, runs cross country and track, and holds the school record for the pole vault. Charlotte explains a couple of her techniques as: when vaulting, she counts her steps to the vault, and when she plays basketball, she listens to the dribbling pattern and lunges in for steals. Said Charlotte to *Yahoo.com*, "I think everyone struggles with something in life. This was my something."

Los Angeles Times sportswriter T.J. Simers wrote about a man named Scott Odom, who was treated for bone cancer at the age of 14 that resulted in the amputation of his leg. Now in his late 20s, Odom plays on a basketball team with other amputees, and also plays against non-disabled teams. He also has a goal of developing a basketball league for amputees. Says Odom, "I lost my leg to cancer, not my dream to play sports. Sure, some people look at me as a cripple. But I'm blessed; I've been given the chance now to make a difference."

Finally ... a story that quickly went viral: Two freshman football teams in Missouri arranged for a running back with Downs Syndrome to score a 65 yard touchdown, and, because of the Internet, the two schools were showered with attention for their sportsmanship and attitude. Describing the overwhelming reaction to the gesture, the players' coach told the Kansas City Star; "It's just amazing how one play can mean so much to one kid, and then to a team, and then to a community."

APPENDIX

Following are just a small number of sources of information available. If you don't find what you need....there's always Google......

YOUTH SPORTS ORGANIZATIONS, FOUNDATIONS AND INFORMATION SOURCES

POSITIVE COACHING ALLIANCE
positivecoach.org

STOP SPORTS INJURIES
stopsportsinjuries.org

TAYLOR HOOTON FOUNDATION (steroid use)
taylorhooton.org

NATIONAL INSTITUTE FOR SPORTS REFORM
fairness.com

INTERNATIONAL YOUTH CONDITIONING ASSOCIATION
iyca.org

RESPONSIBLE SPORTS (LIBERTY MUTUAL INSURANCE)
responsible-sports.libertymutual.com

NATIONAL ALLIANCE FOR YOUTH SPORTS
nays.org

SPECIAL OLYMPICS
specialolympics.org

INTERNATIONAL OLYMPICS
Olympic.org

INTERNATIONAL PARALYMPICS
Paralympic.org

(cont.)

ATHLETES FOR CHARITY *(lists many charities)*
athletesforcharity.com

JIM EISENREICH FOUNDATION
tourettes.org

NATIONAL SPORTS FOUNDATION
natlsportsfoundation.com

BASEBALL COACHING
baseballcoachingtips.net

WOMEN'S SPORTS FOUNDATION
womenssportsfoundation.org

Dr. PATRICK COHN/LISA COHN
youthsportspsychology.com

TEAM UNSTOPPABLE
anthonyrobles.com

WE PLAY MOMS
twitter.com/@weplaymoms

THE EDUCATED SPORTS PARENT
educatedsportsparent.com

TIGER WOODS FOUNDATION
tigerwoodsfoundation.org

SOCIETY FOR AMERICAN BASEBALL RESEARCH
sabr.org

NOTHING'S BEYOND REACH FOUNDATION
nothingsbeyondreach.com

(cont.)

MOMS TEAM
momsteam.com

NATIONAL ATHLETIC TRAINERS ASSOCIATION
nata.org

NATIONAL COLLEGIATE ATHLETIC ASSOCIATION
NCAA.org

GATORADE SPORTS SCIENCE INSTITUTE
gatorade.com

GIRLS ON THE RUN
girlsontherun.org

FUEL UP TO PLAY 60
fueluptoplay60.com

NFL RUSH/PLAY 60
nflrush.com/play60

PEAK PERFORMANCE SPORTS
peaksports.com

SPORTS WEBSITES/BLOGS

Sports Illustrated Kids – sikids.com

Sports Illustrated – si.com

Yahoo!Sports -- sports.yahoo.com

ESPNW.com

ESPN.com

ThePostGame.com

BleacherReport.com

Grantland.com

Rivals.com

Strengthplanet.com

TheBigLead.com

JockBio.com

Getontheline.wordpress.com

SPORTS BOOKS

The Double Goal Coach – Jim Thompson

Why Johnny Hates Sports – Fred Engh

Will You Still Love Me If I Don't Win? – Christopher
Anderson

Talent is Overrated – Geoff Colvin

*Game On: The All-American Race to Make
Champions of Our Children* – Tom Farrey

The Talent Code – Daniel Coyle

*Home Team Advantage: The Critical Role of
Mothers in Youth Sports* – Brooke de Lench

Zen Golf:Mastering the Mental Game– Joseph Parent

Encyclopedia of Sports Parenting – Dan Doyle

The Golfer's Mind – Dr. Bob Rotella

Open: An Autobiography – Andre Agassi

The Courting of Marcus Dupree – Willie Morris

The Ripken Way – Cal Ripken, Jr.

Raising Elite Athletes – Malcolm Conway

Color, Learn & Play -- colorlearnandplay.com

Ready, Set, Play! – Mark Schlereth

The Values of the Game – Bill Bradley

SPORTS MOVIES

"42" (baseball)

A League of Their Own (women's baseball)

Angels in the Outfield (baseball)

Any Given Sunday (football)

Breaking Away (biking)

Bull Durham (baseball)

Chariots of Fire (running)

Dodge Ball

Field of Dreams (baseball)

Happy Gilmore (golf)

Hoop Dreams (basketball documentary)

Hoosiers (basketball)

Jim Thorpe, All American (running)

Jordan Rides the Bus (Michael Jordan documentary)

Kicking and Screaming (soccer)

Little Giants (football)

Long Shot: The Kevin Laue Story (documentary)

Major League (baseball)

Miracle (hockey documentary)

Moneyball (baseball)

Remember the Titans (football)

Rocky (boxing)

Rudy (football)

Slap Shot (hockey)

Space Jam (basketball)

The Bad News Bears (baseball)

The Best That Never Was (Marcus Dupree documentary)

The Big Green (soccer)

The Blind Side (football)

The Boys of Fall (football documentary)

The Karate Kid

The Longest Yard (football)

The Mighty Ducks (hockey)

The Natural (baseball)

Unguarded (Chris Herren documentary)

NOTE: *ESPN has produced a number of documentaries on athletes in their "30 for 30" Series. Information can be found at ...ESPN.com.*

INDEX

INDEX

INDEX

INDEX